WHO THE F#%K CARES?

...ABOUT YOUR ENLIGHTENMENT FANTASY

BY JOEY LOTT

http://www.joeylott.com

Copyright © 2014 Joey Lott
All rights reserved worldwide.

ISBN: 1518697488
ISBN-13: 978-1518697487

Table of Contents

Preface 7

Introduction 9

Escape 12

Idolizing the Teacher 15

Super State 18

The Gods Will Come to You 20

Dark Night of the Soul 23

Fish's Awakening Story 28

Special Powers 35

Loving Everyone 37

Silent Mind 43

The Character and the Play 46

Easy or Simple	48
Stopping	53
Certification of Enlightenment	59
Pointing, Investigating and Belief	63
Surrender	67
Self-Referencing Story	70
I'm Going to Get This!	73
Mystery and Collapse	77
Being in Control	83
The Look of Enlightenment	86
Practice	89
Self-Censorship and Deceit	95
Is Enlightenment An Escape?	99
Trust the Guru	104
Disillusion	107
Maturity of the Seeker	111
What Do You Want to Escape From?	114
Masks and Stories	117

Transition	120
Nihilism	126
The Final Word	130
Happiness Made Simple E-Course	133
Connect With Me	134
One Small Favor	135
About the Author	137

Preface

This book is made up of a series of real-life conversations between two men. We are talking about freedom. Not freedom from anything, rather, the freedom to be as we already are. Which is unboundedness. We are talking about the endless discovery of the vastness, stillness and (dare I say) joy of aliveness.

What we are pointing to throughout the conversations is what is ever-present. We are talking about what others talk about couched in terms of "spirituality." Yet here we talk about it as simply and directly as we can. These conversations are casual. They are approachable. And they are crude.

So be warned. If you are one of those people who includes the phrase "f-bomb" in your vocabulary because you are easily offended by words, or if you find that listening to a Richard Pryor stand-up routine is challenging rather than enjoyable, then this is not the book for you. Please read no further. Really. I mean it. Please stop reading right now.

Okay. You've been warned.
Fuck. Fuck. Fuck. Fuck.
That's just a short preview of what follows.
Oh, and by the way...Motherfucker.
Yes. Really.

Why? Because aliveness knows no bounds. And if you're looking to be happy and serene in your "spiritual safety zone" then there's plenty out there for you. Go read Eckhart Tolle. (Although, I guess even Eckhart Tolle is a bit radical these days. I mean – gasp - he admitted to trying LSD!)

So here is a different offering. Here is an exploration of what already is without much talk of turiya or ananda or any other technical terms borrowed from other cultures and philosophies. I suspect that we're actually pointing to the same thing, but we're talking about it using the language of American men in 2014.

Introduction

I met Fish a little over three months ago. And yes, that really is his name. Well, actually, it's the abbreviated form of his last name - Fisher. But as is common among ex-military-professional-diver-fighter-trainer types, he prefers short, punchy, and to the point. Fisher won't do. And his given name? Fuggedaboutit.

Fish initially contacted me to thank me. He'd read a few of the books I'd written, and apparently they helped to shed some light on his experiences. I replied politely and sincerely. And that may have been that. Except then Fish noticed that I had liked a video on YouTube on the subject of Indian club swinging and he happens to know the instructor in the video. Fish used to run fitness courses in Hawaii. You know the sort. Boot camp-style with lots of yelling and bodyweight stuff and probably lifting and dragging heavy things like tires filled with sandbags. Fish was the one doing the yelling.

So anyway, Fish struck up a conversation about Indian clubs and kettlebells and stuff like that, and then next thing you know, we were talking on the phone about what the hell happened to him more than a decade ago.

Fish was walking across the parking lot on his way to run one of his courses. He was prepared to yell at people to motivate them to "be all that they can be." (I'm mixing up my slogans here, of course. Fish was a Navy Diver, and he'll be the first to tell you that Navy Divers are the best in the history of the world.) And in an instant, "between one step and the next," as Fish says, everything fell away.

For those of you who are unfortunate enough to be spiritual seekers, this sounds like a dream come true. But you should be careful what you wish for. Because for Fish, this falling away was so devastating that he found himself drinking heavily on and off for the next decade, trying to deal with the loss of self.

I was intrigued by Fish. I found him to be likable and fun to talk with. And there was something about his story and his voice that I felt could be valuable to those who are seeking something more, something better.

I wondered how many ex-military, macho, grab-the-world-by-the-balls-and-choke-it-to-death sort of guys are out there, looking for salvation, looking for truth, looking for something, but feel completely unserved by the popular spiritual scene. Fish has something to say to those people. Or anyone else who is just plain tired of the same old clichés. Hell, I sure would have appreciated some directness five or ten years ago.

So we hatched the idea to record some phone conversations and see what happened. I recorded and then transcribed them. And these are what you will read in this book. We had four conversations. And then we broke them up into digestible, thematic chunks to make them more readable. Because we knew that otherwise your head would probably explode from trying to read too much brilliance all at once.

As you read, you will probably notice that Fish and I speak differently about the experience of freedom. There's a very good reason for that: all experience is subjective. The experience of freedom is no exception. The experience is ultimately unimportant other than that it can point to something nearer than experience. So as you read, try not to reconcile the differences in the ways that we each speak about the subject. How we conceptualize or speak of something is necessarily different just as our subjective experiences are necessarily different. And yet, finally, what all of this points to, if you're willing to receive it, is the truth of freedom, which is what includes all of it, including all the differences. And believe it or not, you already are that freedom.

While it doesn't come through in the transcripts, you should know that we were laughing at ourselves and our own apparent follies the entire time. Because as horrific and painful as it may have been, looking back now it's pretty darn funny. Like Fish says, now "We can make fun of ourselves for believing in Santa Claus as kids." Similarly, we can now make fun of ourselves for all the ridiculous things we did - like trying to suck our semen up our spine in order to improve our spiritual power. Or believing that we existed as separate selves.

We laugh throughout. But we're not laughing at you. Well, at least not too much. We have deep compassion for the suffering and the exhaustion of the search for something else, something better. We know well the addiction of trying to improve yourself, to feel better, to avoid your problems.

And our hope is to offer you something unique - a fresh look at what suffering is and what freedom is.

Escape

In this conversation Fish and I talk about the underlying foundation of suffering. However we may conceptualize suffering, and whatever the specific manifestation of suffering, it is always predicated on the assumption that there is something other than this, which is appearing right now.

We normally conceive of what is happening right now and who we are right now as being deficient in some way. We compare our idea of now to our idea of what we believe has previously happened or what we imagine could happen, and then we mistakenly imagine that this right now is not enough. And the way in which we imagine that we can solve this imaginary problem is to escape from this to something else - something better.

J: So, yesterday it got clear to me what it would be really nice to talk about during this conversation - as a broad container or context for the conversation. It occurred to me that often the whole pursuit of enlightenment, or however we fantasize about that, whatever terminology we use, is actually a fantasy about escaping from all the unpleasantness of life.

F: Sure. It's just another form of escape like drinking or drugs. You just want to get away from this shitty situation you're in while avoiding the truth, which is that you're the center of all your problems. There's no escaping that. So when you pursue enlightenment you want to be this wonderful enlightened person minus all the bad habits and all the attributes that would make you a non-enlightened, shitty person.

J: Yeah. And you want to have all the circumstances of life that presently seem to be out of your control within your control, or at least just work out the way that you want them to. So that it's always pleasant.

At least that was my fantasy. Even though I didn't think about it clearly. It was just this vague fantasy that what I was pursuing was going to give me, in the future, an escape from being sick, from pain, from unpleasant relationships, from worrying about money. I imagined that everything would always work out exactly how I wanted it to, and it would be easy-going, smooth sailing, no problems ever.

F: It would be the easy life.

It's hard because we get pulled into that illusion. We see guys like Ramana Maharshi who seemed the consummate always-at-peace-no-matter-what kind of guy. Even when he was sick and dying, he was still walking around, never complaining about anything. He was okay with everything.

And then you see the more modern, hippie era, the more cultish era, where everything is just one giant party.

I used to believe that once I woke up I would be like that movie "Limitless," and I'd be operating with 100 percent of my brain. I'd speak Spanish. I'd be a Jiu-Jitsu black belt. I'd have all these wonderful powers. Money would just come my way. And people would just buy me dinner.

That's really what we're looking for.

J: That's exactly it. That's the fantasy.

F: Heaven forbid you should want to go through some sort of traumatic event and the whole system resets. You want the awakening of Eckhart Tolle, but you don't want to go through the complete psychotic break that he went through. You want cool stuff without being schizophrenic or without being in a gunfight or some of the other traumatic events that people go through. You want the robe and the silk shirts.

J: You want the followers.

F: You want Steven Seagal to come to your house so you can share stories and get fat together.

Idolizing the Teacher

We've all done it at some time or another. We idolize the teacher or, at the very least, the teaching, because we want to believe that we've found the one true way that will deliver us from evil - or at least take away our problems.

In this conversation we explore the error of believing that the teacher or the teaching is, as you believe it is. Because the teacher and the teaching are actually nothing. Truly, there is nothing there. And a truthful teacher or teaching merely points you to yourself as you are. Ultimately, they point to the emptiness and the aliveness that is your true nature. This cannot be found because it never was lost. It cannot be earned because it is what you are.

This is a bit like the story of the laughing Buddha Hotei who pointed to the moon. The teacher or the teaching is the pointer. Fixating on the teacher or teaching is to miss what is being pointed to.

J: Recently I got a scathing response to something I had written. The person believed that I had dissed Eckhart Tolle and Ram Dass, and that was apparently upsetting and unforgivable.

So we have this idea that you can't touch these guys. Like Jesus. Heaven forbid that you ever suggest that it's just a fantasy.

I mean, I don't know. How do I know what Eckhart's experience is? Maybe he's the savior. Maybe he's not. But really, who cares? The point is that you will never know. Your idea is a fantasy. You're worshipping a golden calf. When all along, right here, true freedom is looking you in the face.

F: I think what a lot of people do is put these teachers on a pedestal, and they aspire to be just like the teachers. So when someone says they don't believe everything that Eckhart or Ram Dass or Deepak Chopra says, then they're essentially insulting the believer.

"I believe in this guy. You say he's full of shit. You must be saying I'm an idiot."

J: But it's even deeper than that. We are so attached to the fantasy that you don't even have to say that this other person is a liar or wrong. All you have to suggest is, "I don't know, you don't know, nobody knows." That's then often enough to freak us out. It feels very threatening because we hang everything on the fantasy that this person is right and they're going to lead us to salvation, and we're going to get to have endless orgasms and be happy forever; everyone's going to adore us and we'll never have to deal with any of the ugliness of life.

And my experience is that actually, the ugliness of life continues. The only difference is that before there used to be an idea that there was a possibility of escaping it, whereas now there's a realization that there is absolutely no possibility of escape. This is exactly what is happening right now.

There's another little bit in there, which is the realization that I can't find a boundary between me and what's happening - whether what's happening is the best of times or the worst of times. And so the whole idea of a separate me who is experiencing these things - as if this is my experience - and then the delusion that can come from that,

that I can control it and change it - I just can't believe it anymore because I see that there's only this. The idea that there is a separate me from this isn't believable any longer.

F: Yeah. And for some people it's that sort of intuitive understanding that there is no separation. And then for other people it's like a math equation that they feel they have to figure out. But once it's pointed out that, "Look, man, whoever is getting upset here or insulted or defensive or angry, that's really, at best, a cartoon character. You're really not that."

And once that clicks in - from my experience - once I saw it, I just found that I wasn't so engaged because I saw that it wasn't really threatening me directly.

Sometimes that's the crappy part of it, articulating this to people. Some people get so worked up because they believe in one person's description of this. And they believe that one person's version is better than another person's version and if that's challenged, their personal World of Warcraft character is offended. There's really no need to defend a cartoon character unless you really believe that your imaginary character is better than mine, which we all know isn't possible because mine is bad ass and yours sucks.

I think it would be helpful if we understand that the teacher or author is just interpreting a perspective that nobody except himself or herself can understand. I'll never see things the way you see them, and you'll never see things the way I see them.

Sadly, I think people get so worked up defending their favorite teaching that they can't or won't see the attachment that's causing the problem.

Super State

One of the most common misconceptions that we seem to have is that it is possible and desirable to experience some sort of sustained (read: maintained forever) state of perfect bliss. And we imagine (wrongly) that this fantasy state is what freedom is.

The reality is quite different. The reality is that freedom includes everything, not just nice things. And, importantly, freedom is what is already always the case. So if you have to do something to attain a state in the future, then that state is not freedom. Freedom is what allows for all states, including the state that you want to get away from.

In this conversation Fish and I briefly talk about the misconception of the possibility and desirability of a super state in which everything is going to be different (read: better) all the time.

J: That's one of those other fantasies that there's going to be some sort of super state where everything is going to change. Like I'm going to become enlightened and then I'm going to just see rainbows all the time.

So if somebody asks me, "So what do you see?"

I just see this. It's the same as before. I can't tell you it's the same as what you see because I don't know what you see. But my experience of what I see now and what I used to see is essentially the same. I mean, I do see rainbows on occasion in the sky when it's raining.

But otherwise it's not like light is pouring out from everything and it's not like Jesus is hanging out next to me and we're just shooting the shit all the time. It's exactly the same as before. It's just that the delusion of some other possibility other than this has collapsed. So I'm not actually concerned about what I see and making what I see better and will I see rainbows in the future. Because who cares? It's just another fantasy.

F: The frustrating part can be the competition with some people to see whose version of reality is better. But we're still using words to describe something that cannot be described.

A funny thing about living in Hawaii is that the gurus who live there make themselves so inaccessible that if you don't have a lot of money you can only talk to the disciples.

So you talk to these people, these followers and get their interpretation of someone else's interpretation. I talked to one lady, and she was obviously very "advanced" on the spiritual path. I wore board shorts and she wore clothes from the sixties, so I obviously didn't know anything.

During our brief conversation she told me that she sees photons and auras - she made it like she saw quantum physics when she saw people. And I was like, "What, did you get Lasik? I see dogs and people I care about. I don't know what you're looking at."

But that was part of the cult of personality. The group she was with had told themselves that to be happy and to be in this specific state they had to feel certain things and see things a certain way, and that was the key to happiness.

I looked at her and her friends and I was like, "Hey man, whatever makes your day better."

Of course, my approach was a little more aggressive. But that's my personality.

The Gods Will Come to You

For those of us who have found ourselves reading classical (and sometimes even authentic contemporary) descriptions of so-called enlightenment (which is to say, the discovery of yourself as you already are,) we encounter some rather fanciful descriptions. Of course, there is an abundance of descriptions of experiences that have nothing whatsoever to do with true freedom - lights, energies, etc. - that many confuse with descriptions of freedom. I'm not talking about that here. Rather, I'm referring to what I believe to be authentic descriptions of true freedom, which is already your true nature.

In these descriptions we hear about things such as perfection, equilibrium, purity, tranquility, and so forth. It is easy to confuse these descriptions and believe that something needs to change in order for freedom to come about. Yet the truth of freedom is already all that is. So even though these descriptions and pointers are quite accurate in many ways, we can twist and contort them to signify something else, which perpetuates suffering.

In this conversation Fish and I talk about how as long as we go on searching for our ideas of what freedom might be then we will overlook the ever-present truth of freedom. And ironically, when we cease to look for our fantasies about what freedom might be then we discover the freedom that we already are. This is the freedom in which all that is comes home.

J: I used to read as much as I could stand of the scriptures and the Yoga Vasistha that goes on and on about how wonderful enlightenment is, how all the gods will come to you when you are enlightened and so forth.

Now what I find is that I can actually see the truth of all of that stuff in my own experience. But it's so simple, it's so ordinary. It's exactly what's always been happening. It's just that before I interpreted it all to be something, whereas now I see that there's nothing to interpret. It is possible to simply receive everything without interpretation.

And I think that a lot of that language is something that we can get hung up on, and then we think that it's all something so special. And it's not. It's just that when you realize that there isn't anything else then everything actually is, in a very ordinary way, a miracle. I mean, wow, this is happening.

Everything just becomes effortless. That's all. There's no longer any need to pursue any of that. And so it actually is true, in that sense that the gods do all come to you because you're not pursuing anything anymore. But it's already what is happening. Because the gods are just the miracle of what is happening, which is all being received in the aliveness that I am or you are. That's all. Nothing extraordinary at all.

F: Yeah, when we stop running around and looking everywhere but here then it hits us, "Oh, it's been here the whole time!" It's a very simple yet profound realization that it's been in front of our face the whole damn time. We get too wrapped up in looking to this guy or girl to teach us, or this video, or this retreat, or we've got to buy these beads or buy this crap to see that it's been here the whole time.

It is a simple realization. There's nowhere to go. Nowhere to be.

With that realization you know that this is perfect just as it is because there isn't anything else anyway. Then it's like, "What the hell am I trying for anyway?"

To borrow a phrase from you, it's simply this. Of course, you have to say this really slowly, like it has some kind of deep meaning.

J: t....h...i...s....

Hmmm. Didn't really have the effect I was hoping for. Oh well.

Dark Night of the Soul

I used to be a know-it-all. In discovering myself as I am I discovered that I know nothing. There is no possibility of knowing anything. And truly realizing that knowing anything is a complete impossibility is liberating. There is nothing to know because there is nothing happening and no one to have any knowledge. Knowledge is, like all things, an instantaneous appearance and disappearance, a seeming movement in the unboundedness that I am.

Still, that doesn't stop curiosity. In fact, I find that with the collapse of the illusion that knowing anything is possible (or that there is anything to know) that I am more curious than ever. It's natural and effortless to be curious because everything is a mystery and because curiosity is totally open. Curiosity is inherently satisfied. There is no compulsion to solve anything or figure anything out. Curiosity is just open looking and exploring. It's play. Like we used to do as children. It's delightful.

So one of my passions is helping those who wish to discover themselves to see for themselves that they already are true freedom. And in that work I am always curious. How does one discover oneself as one already is? This is a mystery that I explore moment to moment. It is endlessly fascinating.

One of the questions that I explore is this notion of a dark night of the soul. What I've noticed is that it seems as though in order to see yourself, as you are you must stop looking for something else. And that *seems to require a certain maturity. Because normally we are willing to keep looking elsewhere, even if it is horrifically painful to do so, as long as we feel that we have some viable alternative to looking right here where we are.*

I imagine that this is because we have mistaken ourselves to be what we are not (separateness,) and we have mistaken what we are (unboundedness) to be a deadly threat. And so we are absolutely terrified to simply acknowledge ourselves as we are.

So my question is, is it necessary to "bottom out" before being willing to see yourself as you are? Is there a dark night of the soul process (in appearance) that we go through?

This is all just curiosity. In truth whatever happens is what happens. And there's no possibility of knowing or controlling. All the same, this makes for interesting conversation. And here, in this conversation, Fish and I get to this discussion of the dark night of the soul in a roundabout way, covering some other ground along the way. Fish starts heading in what seems like a totally different direction, and then brings it back around to the dark night - or dark knight, as he prefers to think of it.

F: You hear a lot about these cults where people crash. And all of a sudden they see the ugly truth about the leader. I put a lot of responsibility for people's suffering on the leaders and gurus themselves.

J: Yeah. Me too.

F: These teachers should step up and say, "Listen. I'm not God. I'm just pointing to what is already here."

J: You know, I try to be nice about it because the truth is that I don't know. I've got a very open mind. Anything is possible. And maybe, just maybe, some of these people are telling the truth. Like maybe Adi Da really was the Avatar, and maybe he really did experience this super reality. I don't know. It's possible.

I kind of doubt it, though.

And so in as nice and an open-minded way as possible, I really don't have a lot of tolerance for a lot of the bullshit that goes on in so-called spiritual circles.

Some of the so-called spiritual teachers are just so far out there and so full of bullshit that it's obvious that there's just some sort of egomania going on there. Then many teachers seem pretty genuine. They are offering something that seems really truthful, and they're doing it in a way that by and large seems genuine.

But then there's still always this mystique there. We're allowed to imagine that the teachers really are special in some way. Like they shit roses and have God's direct phone number or something like that. And I wonder why? What's the purpose? Why not just cop to reality, which is: "Hey, I'm not Swami Babanandaji. I'm just Bob. And I shit like everybody else. And sometimes I get sick. And I have preferences. I don't really like crab. And I like sexual orgies."

Why not just admit to it all? That's what baffles me. If you've been through this whole painful search and have really, honestly discovered how simple it all is, then why complicate it at all? I wouldn't even want to maintain that whole image. Because then you've got to hide so much. And I don't know why anybody would want to do that. I'd much rather just be totally honest about all of it.

F: The shitty part of this is that nobody's going to follow a normal, average guy.

J: Yeah, well, that's true.

F: "What do you mean Fish runs a bulldog rescue and is training to be a welder and he wrote a book on spirituality? That's bullshit. If he was really a teacher he'd be at home giving teachings."

No I wouldn't. You want to come over and listen? Then pick up all the dog shit in my yard.

J: Mr. Miyagi style.

F: Yeah. I mean, I'd be cool about it. It's not all about dog shit. I've got bushes that need trimming too and there are always push-ups you can do. If you're going to be a seeker, you might as well be strong too

But we want teachers to be special. So if someone tells their friends that they've read Joey's book, then their friends will say, "Who the fuck is Joey? I've never heard of him. He must be a nobody. He doesn't have his own ashram."

The image that we have of the guru or teacher only builds up our own image of being so smart and wise and spiritual that we picked the right one out of all of the teachers out there. The myth of the teacher becomes more important than the message.

I know that was a long way round back to the dark night of the soul. But that's why I think there a few things that can lead a lot of people to have the dark night of the soul. For one thing, you've built up this image of this whole new world when you wake up. But it's nothing like that. You realize that your shitty life up to now is going to continue to be shitty until you stop doing shitty things. This awakening process doesn't mean all of your problems go away. The analogy that I used to like was the one of the fan - the electricity is going through the fan, and even after you unplug it, the fan blades are still going for some time. So your habits are still going to continue until they don't.

On top of that, if you're following a teacher and suddenly he or she isn't who you thought they were, there can be massive doubts as to your own choices. What else have you fucked up?

It's like getting sober. It's not like you call people up and say, "Hey, I'm sober now. So now I don't owe you any money."

J: More like now you definitely need to make good on your debts. You don't have the excuses any longer.

F: "Now you get a job, loser." You still have to deal with problems.

For me that was the crushing part. I thought it was going to be this wonderful, magical thing. I was going to walk around and have awesome experiences and know wise people. But it wasn't anything like that.

J: So that's an interesting thing that just occurred to me as you were speaking, which is that when we're talking about the dark night of the soul, whatever that really means, I kind of went through that prior to this discovery. And it seems like you want through that after.

I've been very curious about this lately. I don't expect that I'll ever figure it out. And that's fine. But I've been very curious to know what is the role of the dark night of the soul? Is it necessary?

Your story, in a way, provides a compelling argument that it is necessary. Even after you had this awakening - it's like, "Well, let's just check the logs. Nope! Fish didn't go through the dark night of the soul yet. So now he's got to go through it."

Of course, it's nothing like that. More likely, if there actually is any such phenomenon then it's just a matter of all the ways in which we've mistaken ourselves to be something else falling away. Which can be scary and potentially quite unpleasant.

But only for the one that we've mistaken ourselves to be. Because finally, it's clear that nothing is happening.

Golly. Good luck figuring that out.

Fish's Awakening Story

In this conversation, Fish and I talk about his awakening story. Of course, it's just a story. And experiences are just experiences. They don't mean anything. So don't read anything into this.

But at the same time, I really love this story precisely because it's so different than the fantasies that many of us have built up. We imagine that our special awakening experience will be absolutely wonderful in every way, followed by an eternity of pleasant experiences.

Fish's story shows just how wrong we can be. Because sometimes, discovering that you are nobody can be devastating.

F: Some people have some sort of traumatic experience after which they kind of figure out what just happened. I've read stories about awakening happening while looking at a mountain and one story about a guy who got blasted by an explosion in war and then spent almost 20 years trying to reconcile what happened. It's never the same and trying to replicate it is ridiculous.

I was sitting and reading and training and spending a lot of time contemplating things and fantasizing about enlightenment. I really felt that one of these days I was going to find the answer and when this awakening occurred, it would be just as I imagined.

But it wasn't like that. Instead, I walked around and wondered, "What the fuck just happened to me?"

I watched my entire life obliterated right there. I had no idea what to do. I didn't have a teacher. I called the Zen temple, and they basically said that there was no way this could have happened. I didn't log enough hours in the temple to have that kind of experience.

So I wanted to know what happened. And how could I function?

J: So for you, you were walking into the gym one day, and then everything just fell away in an instant. Is that what happened?

F: From one step to the next.

I got up late that day, so I wasn't able to sit for my usual two hours in the morning. So I was upset that I hadn't meditated long enough that morning. And then, like I said, from one step to the next it was like someone turned a light switch way up in my head, and everything was clear. And it took just a blink of an eye. The attachment to the personality fell away. I saw the lie that my own story was. Everything was obliterated.

And I walked around dazed for a while. And by "a while" I mean the first year was the worst.

J: Did any of that return?

F: There was a really intense struggle like a bad kid trying to get back into my head. Like something was trying to take back over. It felt almost like a battle in my head. There was nothing I could do. All I could do was just watch. It was like something was trying to reassert itself.

I still had to do all these things in life, but I didn't know how to do any of that stuff. For a long time I just kind of ran on autopilot, which I later realized is just the way it is anyway.

My entire world fell away which, for me, was devastating. I was an alpha male. I was a navy diver. I was a fighter. I was a trainer. And then I realized that was all bullshit. And I was like, "Wow, that's not very exciting. Where are the half-dressed, attractive women worshipping everything I say?"

J: So your fantasy before that was that you would become even more alpha.

F: Oh yeah. I would be the supreme guru. I was going to be the one that was going to show my perspective on everything. I was going to have all the answers, and I was going to tell you what to do.

If you were a Sunday morning Buddhist, and you were into convenient meditation, then I was going to be the one, hardcore guy like Bodhidharma. I was going to tell you to cut your fucking arm off and then you'd come sit in a cave with me. That kind of shit.

J: And then all of a sudden, you realized that you were nothing.

F: If there were a voice in my head it would have said, "Way to go, dipshit."

J: So your strategy for dealing with all of that was to drink.

F: I didn't know how to handle it. I still had the mentality that I was going to try to control this somehow. But there was absolutely no way I was going to control anything ever again. And it was just devastating. My problems were not solved. I really just crashed and there really aren't a lot of problems when you're passed out drunk.

J: So you were drinking heavily.

F: Yeah. I just started drinking because I couldn't handle it. My world didn't become perfect like I thought it would.

J: So at the time you were training full time?

F: I was training full time. I ran a boot camp class. It was very popular. It was hardcore. It was before the modern generation of these sorts of things. I was basically the drill instructor. My clients wanted to be fighters, military special forces and people that just wanted to do kickass stuff. People looked at me as a kind of aggressive role model. At least that's what I told myself.

I took it seriously. But at the same time it wasn't very stressful for me. I had deluded myself into thinking that I was so badass that everything should be easy for me.

J: Well, apparently, it was easy for you. It was just the aftermath that was challenging.

F: Yeah. I don't know if that played a role that I was trying so hard. It's possible that I just tried so hard to "get it" that it was almost like my brain just said "Fuck it, I give up" and then this shit happened. There wasn't anything I could have consciously done to make it happen. I guess it could be like my own Zen koan, but that's just a guess. I really couldn't have planned it.

I honestly compared it to when I was studying Jiu-Jitsu. We all wanted to be in the zone but that wasn't something that you could just make happen. You had to drill something hundreds or thousands of times so that it became second nature. I thought that if I sat long enough and experienced some super state long enough, it would just happen.

J: So you were sitting two hours a day?

F: Between six and eight hours a day.

J: Okay. So during the six to eight hours that you were sitting what was the process and the experience?

F: I just sat. I got into sitting because I knew that something had to change. I had made a lot of mistakes. While I considered myself a badass, I was hurting a lot of people, including myself. So something had to change.

None of the things I did worked. The positive affirmations didn't work. So I wanted to know "What the hell is wrong here?"

I would sit, and it got longer and longer. At about 10 minutes the chatter in my head would die down a little bit. And I'd have different realizations about stuff I had read.

Eventually it became a habit. I got addicted to it. I had to sit at a certain time in a specific spot for a certain length of time. That became my own prison. And if it wasn't like that I would get really pissed.

J: I can relate to that.

F: And then after the awakening, it wasn't that I didn't want to sit, but I literally could not sit. The next day I sat for two minutes and the inside of my head was like a train wreck. I had no idea what I was even looking for anymore. It was all gone.

So that was the process. The sitting lasted for about six months, which I chalk up to my over-aggressive personality.

J: So when you sat, were you just observing whatever happened or were you watching your breath? Was there any format to it?

F: It was a focusing on the breath. The inhale and the exhale. I likened it to working on cars. I thought of a piston. I thought I had to hone my awareness like a laser to observe the turn at the bottom of the breath.

J: So it sounds like it worked, and the trouble is that you ended up cutting off your own arm.

F: To say that it worked is obviously a misnomer. Because everything that you've ever done has led to now, but who knows what caused what?

J: It becomes apparent that it's all equally important. But it's an interesting story to talk about the sitting for eight hours a day because it's unusual.

F: I wouldn't recommend it!

One of my jokes is that while you're busy sitting, your girlfriend's busy getting. Sitting there waiting for a perfect existence while life passes you by. Dumbass.

J: Of course there are worse things you could do. I mean, you've probably done worse things.

F: Yeah.

J: So following that, how long were you drinking and how heavily were you drinking?

F: I started drinking because the train wreck in my head was just unbelievable. It was nothing like what I had read about or thought I was going to achieve. There were periods of intense crying and emptiness and loneliness. There was absolutely nothing I could do and there were times where I just wanted it to stop. Permanently. Drinking was a way to simply pass out or sleep and not have to deal with it.

Eventually, it became a habit. Then I was struggling with a physical addiction to drinking.

J: Was it unpleasant? Did you get sick?

F: Oh yeah. It was to the point where it didn't matter. I was nihilistic for a while. So I wound up in the emergency room a couple of times. The last time the doctor looked at me and said, "You're either really bad at killing yourself or you need to find something better to do." To which I responded, "Maybe, I'm just too tough!" He didn't find it as funny as I did.

The last time I was in the emergency room I had needles in my arms and probes on my chest, and I felt lost and had lost sight of so many things. I looked out the window, and suddenly I no longer identified with being an alcoholic. There was, and still is, a very deep sense of peace and calm.

It wasn't a big deal, just a "No shit, I'm done" realization. No parade, or party and nobody else could see anything different, and unless I told someone it wasn't apparent to anyone.

J: So when you stopped drinking, then what?

F: Like anything else, I had to deal with the aftermath of years of drinking. But I didn't go from being one disaster to another. It was almost as if I kind of settled into this whole thing. I became much more laid back. Things came up, and I had to deal with them but without the craziness.

Of course I still have my personality. But I don't take it as seriously - like I'm this hardcore dude and I'm going to grab the world by the balls. I don't need to get upset anymore. I'm just easy going for the most part.

I wish that I'd had this kind of understanding when it initially happened.

Special Powers

Here's a short conversation where we poke fun at the fantasies that we used to have about how awakening would be some sort of special, better experience. Plus, we joke about some of the crazy things we believed and did in our attempt to attain that specialness.

J: When did you get the golden aura?

F: After I ate enough of Osho O's, I sent away the box tops. Got the certificate and decoder ring and everything. Be sure to chant my name 217 times every day.

J: That's interesting. For me, I prayed to Adi Da, and he said that I must worship him perfectly 108 times. And I did that. And he tapped me on the forehead.

Now I've got the siddhis happening. I've got bilocation and flying.

F: I'm trying to channel my orgasm up my spine.

J: In all seriousness, that whole thing messed me up for a while. I was dead serious about it. Because you read these stupid books that tell you that if you don't do this then you're going to die a miserable death, but if you do do it, then you're going to be a perfected being and it's going to be awesome.

F: I've had experiences with people telling me to withhold my semen because women will steal your soul.

J: I'm soulless.

I used to have really intense neuroses across the board. You know how you hear about people who are concerned that photographs will steal their soul? I thought that if I disclosed any sort of personal information to anybody at any time then it was going to be sort of like that. I could never reveal anything to anybody. As if it was all so precious and special.

It's such a relief finally to just be done with all that.

F: This guy I was training with in Jiu-Jitsu was a Hare Krishna.

J: Interesting. That sounds like the opening of a bad joke.

F: Yeah. Well, he had literature about how ejaculating was really bad spiritually. And so then I left on deployment (on a Navy ship.) And while on deployment as divers we didn't have any specific responsibilities on this particular ship. So there wasn't much for us to do except eat, sleep, work out, watch movies and jerk off.

So the Hare Krishna guy convinced me that I had to put away the Love Sock and withhold to make use of that energy as a fighter. Which sounded good to me. I think it worked because after about two weeks I thought I was going to fucking kill somebody.

The crazy shit we believe will make us better than we are.

Loving Everyone

We've probably all read something or had a conversation with somebody in which the person raises doubts about whether so-and-so is really enlightened because the behavior didn't fit with the accepted model of "enlightened behavior." Or perhaps, if we tell the truth, we've had doubts. We may have wondered if such-and-such is really enlightened because he or she eats meat or wears make-up or acted impatiently or said an unkind word. Or maybe we expected a certain "energy" or a special look in the eye.

I've got good news and bad news. The good news is that enlightenment is a bogus concept and there is no such thing as enlightened behavior. So we no longer have to burden ourselves with the stress of trying to figure out if someone is enlightened - including ourselves.

The bad news is that since there is no such thing, then there's no longer an escape from what is here. There's no longer any possibility of becoming something else, something better. There is no possibility of becoming enlightened and suddenly being a better version of yourself.

Actually, I guess that was good news too. So maybe it's all good news.

In this conversation Fish and I explore the misconception that upon discovering the freedom that we are, we should automatically be all loving. Actually, I'd say that this discovery reveals the truth of real all-lovingness. The truth of real all-lovingness is the complete acceptance and reception of everything exactly as it is, which includes all apparent *emotions. So ironically, the discovery of yourself as you already are, which is unbounded freedom, is the end of the futile attempt to exclude any apparent emotion, thought or anything else. True freedom reveals that our concepts of love or spirituality or enlightenment are limited. We discover ourselves to be unboundedness, which is what we already always are. No exceptions.*

F: I used to think that after awakening I would love everybody. But actually, I really don't like a lot of people.

J: Oh yeah, I can relate to that one. Which is just totally unrealistic. So no, awakening doesn't mean that I like everyone. Because sometimes people are assholes. And liking or not liking people is just an experience that has nothing whatsoever to do with freedom. Freedom is so free that it welcomes everything, including what we might call love and what we might call hate and everything in between.

It's easy to get hung up on thinking that behavior or attitude or thoughts or feelings have anything to do with freedom. But that's because we mistakenly believe that freedom is personal. Like I get to have my personal freedom. But that's just silly. And discovering yourself as you are reveals that what you are is unbounded, not a person. Which is very liberating. Because it frees you from the crazy notion that you should (or could) constrain behavior or attitude or thoughts or feelings in order to appear more enlightened.

So I'll let you in on a dirty secret of enlightenment (which, of course, you already knowwhich is that I can be as petty and defensive and angry as the next person. If there's any difference now, it's just that I don't have any sense that any of that belongs to me.

Here's an example. I wrote a book about recovering from extreme sound sensitivity - as in feeling a homicidal rage when hearing people chew - which, believe it or not, is a problem that a lot of people have. In the book I share a novel approach that I used to help solve the problem.

The other day, someone wrote a 1-star review of the book, and the review had absolutely no substance, offered no genuine or honest critique. The reviewer then proceeded to slander my person. And I'll tell you what. I didn't feel loving feelings about that. Why should I? I have no delusion that I should feel only a very narrow set of spiritually correct feelings. In fact, I have no problem with whatever feelings happen. Because they're nothing to do with me.

F: I'm with you on the chewing thing. When I hear people crunching ice loudly, I have to remind myself that water boarding is illegal. And I agree with the mystique around enlightenment. It seems to me that with this stuff people take a lot of things very personally. Like it's their responsibility to save the world from making the same decisions that they have made, even with something as simple as reading a book. I think a lot of this comes from not seeing the simplicity in it and the safety in hiding behind obscure bullshit.

J: So I was thinking what is that all about? And it seems to me that it's a cynicism that is borne out of a sense of isolation. Because it seems that there is no one who gives a fuck about you. At the end of the day you're all alone. And the world is pretty difficult to navigate. As long as you've got your health and some luck, then things might seem tolerable. But the slightest little slip here or there and you're totally fucked.

F: You're right. I used to say this to my buddy when I did commercial diving in Hawaii. He took the burden of the shop very personally and everything was a life crisis for him. He took a lot of things so seriously that it caused him a lot of suffering.

The owner was a businessman, and we were basically expendable hires. So I would tell my buddy that even if we quit the shop would still run tomorrow. If something happens to you or me then maybe our personal worlds might stop, but the rest of life will continue. He was also ex-military and believed that he could save the world, just like I did. But when your belief in controlling an objective world out there is obviously bullshit, it can be maddening. He didn't warm up to the notion.

I mean, is there an objective reality out there? No. But in a relative reality, you know the one that we eat, sleep and shit in, the world will keep on going. Just like it has for 6000 years according to New Earthers.

J: Has it been that long? I thought it was only 5774 years. Time flies!

F: I thought it was just 43 years. That's how long I've been around! That's all that matters.

So I had sent you that question about is there true love for everybody and the differences between relative love and absolute love or non-dual love of whatever the cliché term is now. And I think that a lot of the confusion is that the language is specialized. It's like dealing with someone in a medical profession or any field of expertise. There's a certain lingo for each profession and that's how those people communicate with each other.

So when you're new to all this stuff and you haven't read all the books and memorized the Bhagavad-Gita then words like love and hate and ego really throw you for a loop because you have no idea what the other person is referencing. You're reading a chapter from another culture and thinking you understand the whole thing.

J: I actually think that it may be worse for those who have memorized the Bhagavad-Gita and all that. Because they're deeper in. They have a larger investment in the fantasy about what all of it means. And so then they may be wondering, "Where the fuck is the love?"

Because a lot of that stuff does talk about love and bliss and perfection and dispassion and a lot of other concepts. I think it does throw people because then they go searching for this thing they imagine that the author intended.

But I believe that if the author is authentic in the sharing, then she or he is talking about what is already here - not something else. So it's not about love or bliss or perfection or dispassion that is off in the future and different from this right now. It is about discovering that this right now is actually what you've been searching for.

F: I think most of us have played that telephone game where five people later the original message is something completely different. So just imagine the little changes that can be made thousands of years later after an epic like the Bhagavad-Gita was sung and passed down. Nobody's going to keep that right. Things change over time. And we put our own spin on somebody else's translation. Imagine being the cover band for the Gita.

J: You know that joke about the monks, right?

F: Which one?

J: The new monk arrives at the monastery, and he gets assigned to copying the bible. He notices that all the monks are copying from copies. So he goes to the head monk and says, "I have some concerns about copying from copies. What if someone made an error in copying somewhere along the way, and we don't even know about it? Wouldn't it be best to copy from originals?" Seeing the sense in this, the head monk goes down to the archives. When hours have gone by and he hasn't returned, another monk goes searching for him. He goes down to the archives and he hears the head monk weeping. "What's wrong, brother?" he asks. The head monk turns to him with tears in his eyes and replies, "It says celebrate!"

And I think this really is the crux of the whole thing. This is what we get hung up on. We have these fantasies about what life will be like when we've arrived at our destination - whatever that is. You know, such as we've prayed to Jesus enough or we've meditated enough or we've chanted the names of God enough or we've fed enough orphans then something really wonderful and extraordinary and completely unlike right now will happen.

F: It's crazy because we create the end goal and then at the same time we impose the obstacles to that goal. Maybe if someone tells you that you have to pray 10,000 times a day then you might think that's just stupid. But then if this other guy tells you that you have to do 500 squats then that may make sense. But that's just because of your perception or preferences.

Once you wrap your head around the fact that you're the one making the rules and you're the one getting in your own way then it's a whole different ball game.

But people don't want to believe that they're getting in their own way.

"There's just no way I'm the one that's messing this up. It's the book's fault! Fuck Fish!"

Silent Mind

Many of us have picked up the notion that we should have the goal of a "silent mind." And then we come up with lots of ideas about what that means and what that experience might feel like. Normally we imagine that it means the absence of thoughts and perhaps even the absence of phenomena altogether. Which is, in my view, a complete misunderstanding.

Ultimately, of course, it becomes impossible to find a mind, thoughts or even phenomena. But at the same time, all of these things seemingly appear. So having a "silent mind" isn't about changing or controlling the appearances to get them to fit with your idea of what that means. Rather, it simply points to the ever-present reality of what you are, which is inherently silent. What you are is so completely silent that it allows for all apparent phenomena without any interference.

So in this conversation Fish and I explore this theme of the silent mind.

J: The trouble is, though, that we believe that this is not enough. And it feels like it is not enough. It feels miserable. It feels like if I have to sit here in the nastiness of my life then I'll die. But actually, that is the way. As far as I'm concerned, the way is to finally set aside the fantasies and be with what is here.

But the trouble is that it seems like what is couldn't possibly be it. Because I remember that I was always keeping myself busy. I was working or meditating or going shopping or hanging out with friends. And where there were moments when I wasn't distracted enough - I'd be sitting in my apartment thinking, "What the hell am I going to do?" - I'd then start to feel more and more uncomfortable. I'd find something - anything - to do to distract myself.

I think that's the obstacle. For me the obstacle was that I saw that as the problem. I never realized that it was the opportunity. That is the gift. That is the gateway. That is the invitation to what it is that I wanted all along. I just didn't realize it. Because I thought it was horrible. That was the thing to get away from.

F: For me, when I started sitting I saw how the mind never, ever shuts up. It never stops talking. It never stops with the commentary. There's just always some sort of chatter going on. Most of the time we stay busy, so we're blissfully unaware of that voice. Then when we sit still for a minute - I know some people who can't sit still for two minutes - we hear the insane asylum in our heads. We feel we have to do something to get away from the noise and that means not sitting still and focusing on fantasies.

So the few people that talk to me - a lot of people don't talk to me because I'm so abrasive and they think I'm going to make fun of them - they say, "My head won't stop talking." And I say that it never will.

J: So that's my question to you then. Do you find that it stopped for you?

F: No. It never shuts up.

J: That's another major hang up. We hear a lot of these teachers speak about a silent mind.

F: But if you break that down, then what is the mind? It's just a stream of thoughts. That's all it is. Just thoughts. You can try to find the gap between thoughts or you can be involved in martial arts (or anything else) and have the experience all of a sudden that there are no thoughts. And then you can fall into that trap believing that you can have no thoughts and just react like a wild animal all the time.

There is still thinking, but we can also break that down. Are objects thoughts? What about the thinking process do we want to shut up? Creating objects or your stupid narrative?

J: For me it's just a matter of exploring with curiosity. And in that sort of open curiosity everything unravels. What I find is that whatever words we use can be misunderstood. If someone speaks of a silent mind then this may simply be a way of describing your true nature, which is inherently silent. That's always the case for everyone. But that doesn't exclude anything. So the appearance of thoughts is welcome just as much as the appearance of the experience of silence. Because both are simply experiences. And as experiences they are appearing and disappearing in the inherent, unbounded silence that you are.

The Character and the Play

When I first learned about Ramana Maharshi's famous "Who Am I?" inquiry, I was earnestly trying to solve this puzzle of figuring out who I am. I started with the assumption that I must be somebody - something separate - something distinct and findable. And so it never once occurred to me during that phase that perhaps the fact that I couldn't find anything might signify that there isn't anything to find.

In this conversation Fish starts by suggesting that the ones that we mistake ourselves to be are but fictional characters. Then we explore how this orientation totally transforms the inquiry. Without the assumption that I must be something findable, something distinct, then we are free to explore what is as it is.

F: I read a quote by Nisargadatta, and he said that you are all just characters in a play and I am not involved. You are just appearing in a play, and that's it.

And life is just that from my perspective. It's whatever movie that it is - comedy, drama, action, whatever. It's just the involvement in the movie that creates the suffering, without realizing that it's not really real. I mean, it's okay to cry at the end of "Old Yeller." If you didn't cry then I'd be concerned that there's something wrong with you.

But don't get so involved. I mean, when we see people getting so involved in the characters and movies that they get into actual fights - we call those people crazy. But we do that with our own characters!

J: That was a big turning point for me. I've never had a massive, dramatic event of falling away or anything like that. But there have been these moments of seeing through aspects of the illusion, or perhaps I should just say that this moment is always the fresh discovery of clarity.

And that was a significant thing for me to actually see that there is absolutely no proof that I am this character. It's only ever been an assumption. The assumption is just because it seems as though, since I am apparently seeing through the eyes of a character that I am this separate person. But really, there's no proof. And actually, upon investigation, it turns out that not only is there no proof, but what I actually find is that I am that which includes the appearances.

When I saw that everything started to unravel. Because everything is an assumption. If you just go back to the primary assumptions then you can discover that there is no evidence whatsoever that any of it is actually fact.

F: Because everything we believe to be true is just a consensus that changes with the drop of a hat. It can be one way today and something completely different tomorrow. So when was it actually true? Was my belief true when it didn't really impact my life and now I've changed? Were my beliefs true when a group of us believed it? Or just when I believed it?

I think that a lot of people add on more and more labels to this without getting to the simplest part of it. That's the awesome thing about all of this, that it's the simplest observation. That doesn't make it easy! Because you spend your entire life being told and believing that you're this or that, so looking through a different lens is a challenge.

Easy or Simple

The discovery of yourself as you already are is utterly simple. It couldn't be any simpler. In fact, it is so simple that any effort whatsoever is too much effort. Because any effort is an illusion. What you are is effortlessness itself, and therefore if you imagine that any effort is possible then you overlook yourself exactly as you are.

You as you are is not hidden. It is plainly obvious. It is what is always already the case. And, strange as it may seem, it is also what is appearing right now. This is yourself. There is no possibility of escaping from it.

But we often complicate this. Because we imagine that this right now could not possibly be it. We imagine that "it" must be way cooler, probably with a better cast and better lighting. And definitely a better lead character. So we set about trying to improve the lead character so that he or she can live happily ever after.

Seriously, though, true freedom, which is your true nature, is already the case. It couldn't be simpler.

The frustrating part is that we mistakenly conflate simplicity with ease. And they are not the same thing. Although being yourself as you are is so perfectly simple that you cannot fail to already be that, recognizing this simple truth is not always easy. Because it seems to go against the entire momentum of everything that we have ever done.

Why? Probably because the discovery of yourself as you already are is the dissolution of everything that you are not. It is the complete end of everything that you have ever imagined yourself to be.

The good news is, of course, that who you have imagined yourself to be never existed anyway. It was only a fantasy. So the dissolution of what never was changes nothing.

Confused yet?

Well, you probably won't be any clearer after reading this conversation that Fish and I had about this very subject of simplicity and ease. Sorry about that.

F: And of course, a writer or teacher could say that it's easy because there's no you to do anything. This is really annoying because there is obviously a me that is suffering and this me is a habit that has been built up my entire life.

J: It's not easy. From my perspective, it goes against the whole lifetime. There's this massive snowball effect of the momentum of a lifetime of trying to get away from this. Because in my experience it feels like it's going to kill you. If you just stop for a second and turn around and actually look at the reality of what's here, it feels as though that will kill you. "Wow. That's going to destroy me. I better just keep going in this other direction. I better keep trying to escape," even though there comes a point when it's impossible to believe any longer. "Wait a second. I'm never going to escape. No matter where I go, no matter what I do, no matter how hard I try it goes with me. I'll never escape it." But still, we try to escape it. Because we don't know what else to do.

So in my view it really is a big deal. It's not easy. I never try to trivialize that because I know how intense that suffering can be, and I know that it's a really big deal. It's not easy to turn around and discover the reality of what's here.

Because it goes against everything that you've ever done in your entire life.

F: The human being as an organism - it's in our survival instinct for there to be a me and a you. It's just human nature. My tribe and your tribe. Sure, we all want to get past that and be one happy-go-lucky non-dual family. But when everything around you is telling you otherwise, it's really difficult to see through that.

I think for a lot of people they just want some peace and happiness. They don't want the full-blown awakening with all the craziness of your life falling away. They just want the good stuff. But of course, you can't control it. "I'm going to dictate the way this enlightenment happens so I can have the peace and happiness and just be a cooler me."

J: I don't think there is any peace and happiness apart from the full-blown thing because otherwise there's always that anxiety that there might be something else, trying to escape from what's here. Not that I'm suggesting that awakening makes a person always peaceful and happy in the way that we think of that. Because fundamentally what I'm pointing to when I say awakening is the discovery that I am that which welcomes everything, including the appearance of peace and happiness as well as the appearance of war and misery. And that doesn't happen to a person. That is just the discovery of myself as I already am. So what happens seemingly to the person is totally unpredictable.

F: Yeah. You know, a lot of people use spiritual pursuits as a sort of life management kind of thing. They want to learn how to deal with things differently and in some kind of spiritual manner as if spouting verses make you less of an asshole. And, you know how you and I have talked about how awakening doesn't make your everyday life better, necessarily. It doesn't really help you as far as business or suddenly turn you into a wonderful person. I guess you do deal with things differently. It's not that it doesn't affect you, but it doesn't necessarily make your life better. Maybe. Maybe not.

I hate those trite t-shirt phrases. "Maybe it will make your life better. Maybe not." But it's true.

J: Although I would say that it is better. Just not better as I had imagined it would be. It's better in a way that has absolutely nothing whatsoever to do with the whole story of me and my life - what I'm doing, where I'm going and how I want to arrange everything. It's only better in a very simple way, which is simply that I'm no longer trying to escape from what is unavoidable, from myself.

F: Because you can't. And that's the whole point. There's nowhere to go. This is the totality, the Tao, etc. And it encompasses everything. So where else are you going to go outside of that to be?

Of course that sort of thing really doesn't help anyone.

J: True, depending on the context. If you just get a book of quotations out of context then it may not be helpful. But then if you have someone asking a question and the person responding to the question answers with, "There is nothing outside of the Tao," and he or she is speaking from authentic experience and knowing, then it could be that such an answer in the right context could be the catalyst.

F: Sure. But then it could be anything!

J: Sure. It could be taking a shit.

F: Yeah. Because we can fall into the trap of thinking that it's going to be something special. I used to fall into that trap. I'd think, "It's going to be this book."

J: The problem is that we are usually looking for an answer. And the answer is not an answer. The answer is just to stop looking for something else. To finally just be with what is actually here. And to discover that - not as a finality - not like you'll arrive and then "ta-da," you're enlightened forever and ever; it's actually just an endless dropping into this. Finally, it's no longer trying to get it. To me, that's the relief. There is no realization. There is nothing to get. It's already here. It's already an endless revelation. You can't do it. It's just that when you stop trying to get it then it is revealed.

Of course, that's exactly the kind of bullshit that is so frustrating to listen to. It's frustrating if you're seeking something. But I'm not sure how to turn somebody around. Because you're right that it's a complete paradigm shift. For 50 years or 40 years or 25 years you're looking through a particular lens. And so that is how you understand everything. And what is required is to completely drop that and turn around and discover what is actually here. But to communicate that clearly and effectively - that's the challenge. Because a lot of the time we are still trying to understand something.

Stopping

I remember reading transcripts of talks with Papaji. And he would instruct people over and over to simply stop. He would say to stop for just "half a second."

And I didn't know what he meant. How do I stop?

When I have conversations with people, sometimes I speak of letting go, which is another way to point to the same thing as stopping. And almost invariably, people ask me how to let go.

So I'm prepared for this now. Because it comes up so often. So I'll walk you through how to let go. First, pick up something in your hand and make a fist around it. Hold your hand straight out in front of you with knuckles up. Then let go.

What effort is involved in letting go?

If you answered no effort then you answered the way that I wanted you to. And ultimately, that's what this is all about - pleasing me by answering the way I want you to. Seriously, though, can you see that letting go is effortless? In fact, all the effort is in the holding on.

Stopping is exactly the same way. You can test this out. Find an open space like a park or a yard or a field. Run. Then stop.

What effort is involved in stopping?

The trouble is that the momentum can make it seem as though letting go or stopping requires effort. That is the illusion created by the appearance of investing in something.

The good news is that you never have been invested. You never did anything. You never could do anything. No investment is possible. Just as you cannot possibly be in your own dream. Sure, within the dream there may be the illusion of investment. But as soon as you wake up the dream is gone. Any apparent investment is gone. And you are not diminished or altered because you never were in the dream.

So the instruction to let go or to stop is not about making the character do anything. It is not about controlling the appearance. It is about discovering yourself as you already are. It is about discovering that you already are stopped. You already are the letting go. Because that is your true nature.

In this conversation Fish and I talk about stopping. We talk about stopping the seeking, which makes it sound like you could do that. But you can't, of course. Rather, it is about the intention revealing your true nature. You never could seek. Any appearance of seeking appears within you.

F: I have experience, obviously, with drinking and then stopping drinking. And so I would compare the seeking to an alcoholic drinking. He's trying to quit drinking. So you don't tell him to just slow down on the drinking. Eventually you have to stop drinking.

So the seeking is the same thing. You can't just ease up on the books or the sitting. One day you have to actually stop looking. There's no other way around it. You can't just seek on weekends or maybe you'll just seek at night before bedtime. There has to be a complete and utter stopping. Because the seeking is causing the suffering just as the drinking is causing the suffering. So just stop.

That sounds like a real asshole thing to say to somebody, though. "Hey, why don't you just quit?"

J: Ultimately that's it, though. You have to stop. If you want what you say you want then there is no other way. You have to stop. Because what you want is what is already here.

And as long as you're seeking it you'll continue to overlook it.

F: It's the sincerity of the seeking.

If I had known that awakening would be an obliteration of my life, as I knew it, I probably would have thought twice! I had thought it was going to be an easy transition and I had all the fantasies. But if I had known that it would shatter everything that I thought I knew - it was terrifying.

You know, I don't shy away from things like that. I mean, obviously, with my job in the military, I used to fight. I'm not fearless, necessarily. But still, this was a whole other level of terror of nothingness. There was nothing!

Some people say, "Oh, that's what I've been looking for!" And I say, "No. That's not what I was looking for, buddy. I was looking for the bliss that everyone talks about. Not the stark terror of nothingness."

But when you just sit down and you're honest about why you're doing all this stuff - the seeking - for peace of mind, to be a guru, do you really want to give up everything? Not just the bad parts that make you a loser, but all your assumptions.

You don't have to question everything. You don't have to necessarily go through the whole list of beliefs and things like that. At least I don't think you do. But when all that falls away - when that one thing falls away - then it all falls away. You don't get to pick and choose.

To reference drinking again - once you stop the drinking, you can't drink part time. You have to stop the crack. You have to stop the heroin. You can't just use it on the weekends. You have to stop. The seeking has to stop. And a lot of that comes with the sincerity that this is already it right here.

J: That is true. There has to be a commitment that I'm not going to go off seeking any longer. Whatever happens. And that's why I often say to people that in my experience it's about welcoming the things that you've tried to avoid - the things you desperately want to avoid. Because it's easy to welcome the things you want. But it's the things that you don't want that seem to be the problem. It's when something that you don't want happens that you go off seeking. So you can see that pattern and choose to stay here and discover what this is. Because it's not what I've thought it was.

F: Yeah, we're generally not trying to avoid fun situations. Generally, we're looking for something else when things go bad. When you lose your job or when things are going south. That's when you go off seeking.

J: Or just when some unwanted experience of any kind happens, which happens daily. Just some unwanted or uncomfortable feelings, sensation, thought, memory or whatever. Something happens and for whatever reason you're in the habit of assuming that is a problem that you have to get rid of. And that's what triggers the seeking. "Oh shit, not that! Quick! To the books!"

F: Yeah. "To the sitting room! To the beads!"

J: All of which is why for many people awakening is a very unpleasant experience. Because it's like "Oh shit! I had no idea that this too had to be allowed. I was trying to avoid that emptiness or nothingness or the void, and that too has to be included!"

F: Yeah. Like you said, it's embracing all of it. Not just the fun parts. But the shitty parts too.

But then we fantasize about pick and choose awakening. Not an all around "Hey, you've got to accept everything."

Not that you have to, of course. But that's the suffering - trying to pick and choose. It doesn't matter if you accept it or not because it's here either way. The universe, or whatever word we want to use, doesn't require your permission.

J: That's what I usually try to tell people. I say that it's not virtuous to awaken. It's just sane. That's all. It's just the end of the insanity of trying to avoid what is unavoidable. That's it. It's just to recognize that in this moment, just in this moment - I'm not talking about 10 minutes from now - it's actually here, whether you like it or not. Just recognize that it's already here. There's no possibility of avoiding it.

And if you take this opportunity and notice the actuality of what is here, then you can start to see that what is here is you. There is no separation between you and what you've been trying to avoid. You've been trying to avoid yourself. And that's it.

That's why it doesn't have to be pleasant from here on out. It's just the recognition that this is myself. This is it. This is myself. There's no longer that compulsion to attempt to avoid myself.

F: To avoid it or to control it. That was my trip. I was going to wrap my hands around it and control it. My attitude was, I can make the world do whatever I want. To see that there wasn't an outside world separate from me that I could control was a shock.

"You mean the world isn't out to get me?" No. The world doesn't care about you. Your ego story is only important to you. There is no world out there trying to get you.

It's a very twisted path with no template for getting to wherever, which is nowhere.

I'm getting all wise now with my sayings.

J: Yeah. You're catching on to all the lingo.

F: It's because I had a Mountain Dew and I'm all pepped up. A Mountain Dew and a Red Bull.

J: I thought maybe you'd been reading Tony Parsons.

F: That's tonight's reading before bed. That's when I get serious.

J: Then you'll no longer use any personal pronouns. Then it won't be "I see." Instead it will be, "Here it is seen."

F: There is seeing here.

Really? Because there is punching right here!

J: I do not feel pain. Pain is felt here.

F: Bleeding is going on here.

I think another stupid hang up is romanticizing other cultures. We glamorize cultures that we believe are more in tune with nature. But none of that makes any sense to me and none of it will help me see the simplicity of this. I have no desire to make an atlatl or whatever the Aborigines used to hunt with. None of that is relevant to my life at all. All the talk about how great these ancient cultures were only complicates the simplicity of this and, usually, makes us look like dumbasses.

"Listen, babe. I want you to wear this beaver skin and only eat the food I kill with this stick."

"But we live in a town."

"Why do you hate me? Are you jealous of my spirituality?

If I started talking like that then I'd be left all alone, sleeping on a park bench with pigeons.

J: People will want to know what happened to Fish. "Well, he's working on his atlatl."

F: Yeah. I'm working on throwing my atlatl at cans while covered in pigeon shit. Because, you know, that gets me closer to enlightenment.

J: Donate a can to Fish.

Certification of Enlightenment

It is fascinating to me now how I lacked any sort of genuine critical faculty for most of my search. Of course, this makes sense. How could I have? I was always only comparing the relative to the relative. And so there's no possibility of making sense of that. It's like trying to carry water in a sieve. It's totally hopeless.

So along the way I believed a lot of crazy stuff. I followed a lot of goofy teachers who talked about enlightenment as some sort of kundalini experience or an out of body experience or a near death experience or lights or hearing the voice of god. Because I didn't know better.

I got more and more confused. What was I looking for? How could I get it? How could I thoroughly purify and perfect myself so as to be worthy?

In this conversation Fish and I talk about this phenomenon. You know, there are organizations that certify doctors, lawyers, teachers and so forth. You have to have a license to operate an automobile legally. But any Johnny-Come-Lately can set up table and start hawking his or her wares under the guise of "spiritual enlightenment."

So how do you know whom to trust? Are Fish and I frauds? Was Adi Da really the one and only way?

I'll answer the questions. Because I hate to let you arrive at the conclusions yourself. Mainly because there are no conclusions. If you arrive at an answer then you're mistaken. Keep exploring. Because the only answer is the endless openness of true curiosity. When you know that there's no knowing, then you're close. When you know that there's no security then you're closer still. And when you know that there's no one separate from what is happening, then the question and the answer and the seeking collapse into what already is.

The only ones you should trust are those who point you to yourself, who question everything and pull the rug out from under you more often than they give you anything to hang on to. Oh, and I'll add that the only ones who are trustworthy also claim nothing for themselves. Which doesn't mean they won't accept your donations. Fish and I are glad to receive your $10,000 donations for our new ashram. But it's all about god. God and flashy cars. God, flashy cars and retreats in the Caribbean.

J: To that point you made just a moment ago about how there is no certifying authority that authenticates you as an "enlightened master" - it's interesting because I write things, I put them out there, and in everything that I write the offer is there that if you want to, you're welcome to contact me. I'm happy to hear from you. And people take me up on the offer.

I have yet to receive an email from someone stating, "You are an outright fraud. You disgust me. I hate you." What I get are sincere emails from people who are looking for some sort of insight or guidance or something to help them with whatever they perceive to be the problem. And of course, I know that I'm genuine, so there's no problem. But at the same time I become aware through the process that somebody could write some bullshit thing, publish it and people will read that and because they don't know any better - all they know is that they're in pain and this author maybe seems to have some answers - they look to the author as a teacher. And that's kind of disturbing.

F: It's easy to fall into that trap, I guess. Thankfully, I haven't found myself in that. When I ran my classes in

Hawaii, it was just me and a couple of instructors to help. And I realized early on that I wasn't really doing anything. It was just kind of happening and the creativity was coming from somewhere, but it wasn't planned. This was even before I got into Zen or anything like that. I just knew that I wasn't really doing anything.

People would say, "Fish, you changed my life!" And I would say, "Listen, I'm just here yelling at you guys and pointing out that you're being a doofus. You're the one doing all the work." And I would tell you that I see something in you and I'm going to get it out of you, but if you didn't want it to happen it wouldn't happen. I'm not really doing anything.

But I see people who say, "Oh, I'm the best coach. If it wasn't for me then you'd be a loser." They fall into this really massive ego trip without realizing that they're not doing anything. The student or the devotee or whatever is the one giving you permission, so to speak. And even that doesn't come from them. It just arises.

To avoid that trap - I don't know if it's hard or not since I've never really fallen into it - I think you need to see that this isn't something that you own and can give to others. But I can see the allure of followers, I guess. Dirty bums cluttering up your house eating all your food and not showering. Of course, watching the jealousy and the bickering that goes on between followers is always funny to watch.

"I'm the better teacher," or "My teacher is the better teacher." My favorite is tracing the lineage of teachers to you. Talk about arrogance.

J: I don't know if I can even see the allure. For me, kind of like you were saying that you were just yelling at them, you were just observing and pointing out what you notice. And that's sort of what I do if someone contacts me to talk about non-duality. I don't pretend I know the answer. Of course, I can point. But even more than that, I just point out where the assumptions are being made. There are often assumptions within the questions themselves. So I suggest looking to see if the assumptions are true. That's all I do. And it seems to be helpful for a lot of people.

In my own experience, authenticity in the realm of offering support or helping discover what is as it is requires total clarity, ruthless investigation, and heart. I couldn't do what I do in communicating with people if it didn't have all three. I am entirely clear that absolutely nothing is happening. I am ruthless in questioning every assumption. And, as touchy-feely as this is, I know and feel the love that the person I am communicating with is, which is the love that I am. I don't talk about that sort of thing a lot because I think it's sort of distracting. But without the love I don't see that there's any real possibility of honest sharing or pointing. Because I point to the emptiness over and over again, which can be totally devastating because it strips away everything. So I can only do that with authenticity because I know the secret: the emptiness is the love.

Pointing, Investigating and Belief

Along the way, so to speak, some teachers tell us how it is while others prompt us to find out for ourselves. Some tell us that we already are what we seek while others tell us to investigate what we are trying to avoid. So which is the better approach?

In this conversation Fish takes the stance that those who want to be told are losers while the best way is to be pointed and to explore for yourself. But then I pull out the trump card - a Nisargadatta reference - which I think gives me the win. But then Fish says the word "motherfucker," which I believe may give this book the dubious honor of being the first non-duality book to use the word. (Though, to be fair, reportedly Nisargadatta said things that his translators refused to translate. So for all we know the honest translations of his work would have included the word.)

So you'll have to decide for yourself who won: Fish or me.

F: And with this kind of stuff - and of course I have a preference - I don't like to be told what is true. I like to figure things out myself; which is how I wound up sitting by myself, because at that Zen dojo I had been training at everybody wanted to give me the answers. They wanted to spoon feed me the answers or go ask the Roshi, who I later found out was banging the female priests. But I didn't want to be told what the answers were and I sure as hell didn't want to get banged by the Roshi. I want to be pointed in a direction and figure it out myself. Some people don't want to be given the answer. They just need a pointing finger or a guiding question. "Look over here. Ask yourself this."

I did this kind of stuff in my classes. People would come believing they were fat and weak. I would harass them about thinking like that and push them. Some people would get so mad that they would do a pull up just to spite me for calling them fat losers. As soon as they would do it and drop to the ground you could see it in their faces. It wasn't about me making them feel good and telling them they could be strong. They had to feel it for themselves.

What we're talking about is the same thing. We can point in a direction, but the person has to look for themselves.

But some people just want to be told, "This is this. You believe it." So they just say, "He said it and I believe it." There's no questioning. There's no doubt. There's no investigating. There's just listening, memorizing verses and phrases and repeating them.

J: I can see how both can be useful. I read something that was attributed to Nisargadatta. Of course, I'm hesitant to ever say that anyone actually said anything. For one thing, what I read was in English, and presumably Nisagadatta spoke in Marathi. And for another, I wasn't there to actually hear it. But in any case, this quote attributed to him is a nice one that touches on this subject and reminds me of the potential value of belief.

I'm paraphrasing, but it goes something like this: the questioner wants to know how it was that Nisargadatta "got it." And Nisargadatta supposedly replies that his guru told him to remain with I am, and he believed his guru and did as he was told.

F: I think maybe the phrase was something like "you are not what you take yourself to be."

J: Oh, okay, that may be it. So there's value in both the belief and the investigation. One can support the other.

F: Sure. And this depends on the person who is actually seeking, too. I mean, two people can say exactly the same thing, and the one seeking will hear it from one and not the other. You have basically the same thing in a relationship, too. Your wife or husband maybe says something for a year, and then you hear the same thing on television and you're like, "Hey, that's the best thing I've ever heard!"

And they'll look at you like, "Motherfucker. I've been telling you that for the longest time." And you're like, "Well, honey, I wasn't ready to hear it then, but I am now."

J: When Dr. Phil tells you.

F: That's when you find yourself next to a guy covered in pigeon shit at the park.

But when you're ready, you're ready and nobody can force you to be ready. You know how we were talking about how the machismo gets in the way. It's usually when you're not prepared to hear it, that's when you hear it. When you're not trying so hard to listen, this realization just sort of comes into play when you're not trying so hard to get it.

You hear all the stories about how people come up with great inventions and they solve all sorts of problems when they're not trying so hard.

Just relax for a second. It will come. Just relax. It will happen.

Or it won't. It's not always going to happen.

But more often than not, it's when you're least expecting it.

J: Yeah. The trouble is that we're so conditioned to imagine that we do everything that we mistakenly believe that we have to do the relaxation. We have to do the letting go. Which is obviously an impossibility.

So the secret is that the instruction to relax or to let go is really just a pointing to your true nature. You cannot relax. You cannot let go. You cannot stop. Because you already are that. So the instruction is really to recognize your true nature, which is already what is true. And it is not in any way in conflict with the appearance. Because what you are is the relaxation that is so completely relaxed that there is no possibility of resistance. Everything that appears is relaxing into and dissolving into that which you are.

Surrender

Surrender is one of those nice, warm and fuzzy spiritual terms. Just saying the word makes most of us think about being held like a child in his mother's loving arms.

Yet the truth of surrender isn't like that. The truth of surrender is what is already happening - you just don't realize it. Because surrender is the complete welcoming of everything exactly as it is, including the horrific stuff. Surrender means that you're not in control. Because you're not. Because there is no separate self.

And the discovery of the ever-present truth of surrender can be really scary as long as the last vestiges of a belief in a separate self remain. Because we wrongly imagine that surrender is something that happens to a separate self. As though a separate self could or would ever surrender voluntarily to the great unknown.

Fat chance!

In this conversation, Fish and I talk about our discoveries of surrender. The good, the bad and the worse. It's not pretty. But it's liberating. And freedom is what we most deeply desire. Far more than we want our pretty ideas.

F: That's what happened with me. I had planned on it happening at my house. It was going to be fabulous.

Nope! Right before I went to work. Nothing like shaking everything up.

J: I think it has to be like that because the whole - at least for me the discovery is that there is absolutely no possibility of control, not even the tiniest bit. And there's no way you can ever arrive there from this attitude of "I'm going to get it." Because they are antithetical to one another.

I wanted to get it. So I was trying really hard to get it. And then, for me, I had to get really sick. And I was so sick that there was no way to meditate any longer. I tried meditating. I tried qi gong. Forget about it. There was no possibility. I was too weak, and I had no ability to focus on anything like that. I would try and 10 seconds later I would just be done. I couldn't do it.

And then finally, after enough of that, there was a sort of - you know people talk about surrender. Of course, surrender makes it sound like there's someone surrendering. Like there's a choice made by someone to surrender. But it's not like that. The surrender for me was just the discovery that there is no ability to struggle against this. There is no possibility of it. And then that little switch can happen. Of course for you it was very dramatic. For me it was very subtle. There was just this subtle switch. Almost imperceptible. It was like, "Oh shit. I had it all wrong. Total misunderstanding. Complete misunderstanding." Of course I wasn't going to get it! Because the whole context for the attempt to get it was wrong.

F: Yeah. It's just the wrong way to go about it. What I think people hear, but they don't usually understand, is that the you that is supposed to get it is just a figment of imagination. There's nothing you can do. The person is not a concrete thing. The person you think you are is just a flowing of ideas that will change today and tomorrow and the next day. So there's really nothing tangible that can get anything. And you're trying to build something on top of a story. To make your story even better by polishing a turd.

Of course it can't do anything at all. It never has and it never will. That's just the basic gist of it without getting overly complicated. Because it doesn't need to be. That's the bottom line. When it's fully understood that you exist only as a story, or social convention, you see that these things aren't really real and they don't really do anything. So to think that the idea is actually going to accomplish anything, let alone surrender - that's the problem right there. And it's not about praying and counting beads and logging hours in the zazen log, sitting meditation and everything else. It's just getting to the basics of the entire problem.

But we just want to make it super complicated because that adds to the coolness of the story.

Self-Referencing Story

Normally we are unaware of how much we merely assume to be true that isn't actually findable. All that is actually happening is instantaneous appearances and disappearances of whatever appears and disappears in this moment. That is all. But then there's a conceptual layer (apparently) that tells a story about what all of it must mean. And that story is founded upon assumptions.

Everything that you can conceive is the story. Because the story is simply concepts in much the same way that a book is made of words. And like we can become mesmerized by a novel, we can become mesmerized by the story, wrongly imagining that the story is anything other than a work of fiction.

Like a novel, our stories are entirely self-contained and self-referencing. All the proof and evidence that supports the claims of the story is contained entirely within the story. There's no concept outside of that.

So the challenge is to perceive directly, without concepts. And then to let go of perception entirely. And here you discover yourself as you already are, which is that which receives all perception and conception and everything else that appears.

In this conversation Fish and I talk about the self-referencing story.

J: The challenge, I think, is that the story - people don't realize this - but if you really just pause for a moment and take a look, it's obvious that the story is completely self-referential. There isn't anything outside of it. It seems like there is because within the story there's a story about the past and all this shit that's happened. But actually, the story is complete within itself, and it's happening right now. So what happens is that the story supports whatever the belief is. It's going to construct itself around whatever that belief is. If the belief is that I am this person who does shit then the story is going to support that. But when you finally discover that it's just a story and that you are not defined by that story whatsoever, that you are actually none of it, and yet all of it is yourself. Like when you're sleeping and dreaming, you aren't the dream, but the dream is you. You aren't defined by the dream. The dream doesn't touch you. But at the same time, the dream is clearly you. There's no way that it could be anything else.

For me, and we've talked about this before, there was this little thing that clicked, and I realized that I always assumed that I was this body because the body is always here except when I'm in an altered state. But then, to realize, "Wait a second! There's actually no proof that I am this body. It's just something that is happening." That was a big shift.

It's the same with the story. The story is just happening. I'm not that. It was just an assumption. That's all.

F: And you and I can be at the same place at the same time and see two completely different things. And that's part of it. Chipping away at the belief that the story is you. It's not that you're not the story that's the problem. It's the illusion that you are the story. It's not going through your entire life and finding examples of where you didn't have free will or where you didn't choose. That could take forever. You don't need to whittle down every single facet that makes you think you're this story. You just have to question the belief that you're this story. That's it.

Once that's realized then everything that goes with it goes too. It's not a long, drawn-out process where you've done these steps then you've graduated to the next investigative process. It's just, let's get down to brass tacks and challenge this one assumption.

And unfortunately, you know, Ramana Maharshi had "Who am I?" But that gets turned into a mantra that means nothing. And people just repeat it and repeat it and repeat it. I see the guys with the beads, and it's just a habit for them. It doesn't really do anything. It's just something they repeat while walking around. And it's just as bad as saying "I am this. I am that. I am Fish. I am this person." It's the same thing.

It's just questioning that one belief, which is the pivotal one. And when that clicks, everything else automatically is like, "Oh. Well, that's bullshit!"

J: But it's tricky to communicate that. Because people seem to be willing to hear anything other than that. They're just trying to fit it all into their story.

F: Yeah. You have the story and the storyteller and the story listener.

And there is no story other than the one you're making up in your head. But again, people want to add on to their version of what's happening.

I'm Going to Get This!

Raise your hand if you've ever imagined that you were going to get this whole enlightenment-awakening thing. If you haven't raised your hand, then you're in the severe minority. Because that's how we tend to approach it. We figure that we were able to learn multiplication tables and how to read, so we should be able to figure out how to free ourselves from suffering.

The trouble is, of course, that the one that wants to free itself from the suffering is the suffering! So there's no possibility of that particular fantasy ever coming true. The imaginary sense of a separate self can certainly seem to take ownership of lots of experiences. That much seems possible. So it may seem that the separate self can have relatively more expanded and seemingly more liberated states.

But what you most deeply want you cannot get. You cannot have it. Because what you most deeply want is what is obvious in the discovery that there is no possibility of possessing anything. In fact, none of this has ever been yours. None of it. None of the experiences are yours. All that happens is the appearance of experience and the imagined sense that it belongs to someone. You wrongly imagine yourself to be the one that the experience belongs to. That is all. It's all founded on a mistaken assumption. Because actually, there is no proof that there is an owner of any experience. There is only the appearance of experience.

Confused yet?

Fish and I belabor this point here in yet another stunningly brilliant conversation. Prepare yourself to be enlightened by our words.

J: It comes back down to, "Why can't I get this? What can't I do it? I can do other things. I can manage to wipe my own ass. I should be able to do this!" And it's very frustrating. I used to take this approach of I'm going to just sequester myself in a room until I get it. I'm just going to sit here, eyes closed, not move until I get it.

It will never work. Because it's trying to fit the totality into a piece of totality. There's no way it could work. And who's going to own that anyway?

F: Like you said, you're trying to fit the totality into an experience. And your experience is basically an abstraction from the whole. You have a symbol representing the totality and now you're going to chase after the symbol. So there's a symbol that represents your life chasing another symbol that we believe represents the one, the Tao, enlightenment, whatever. The futility is just ridiculous. Once you see the simple aspect of that realization, then you're like, "What the hell is going on here?"

On top of that, we're conditioned to believe that we can achieve anything. We're told that we're these wonderful, smart, brilliant people. And everybody's kid is easily seven levels above everybody else's reading, despite evidence to the contrary pointing to the fact that you're a fucking doofus.

J: Except my kids. My kids are definitely in the top one percent of the top one percent.

F: Yes. I forgot.

People used to come to class with their kids and their kids would do something that a kid would do, like eat some dirt. And I would just look over and say, "That kid's a genius, huh?"

"Shut up, Fish!"

"That's your little Einstein."

You know, we're conditioned to believe that we can accomplish anything. And it strengthens the notion that we can accomplish this (awakening.) While the realization is that I can't do anything. There's nowhere to go. I hate to be cliché about this, but there's nowhere to be.

J: But the problem is that people try to make sense of that as part of their story. So there is a story about me and my life. And that's fine. There's no problem whatsoever with that as far as I'm concerned.

And people - and I did this to be sure - they're trying to fit it all into their story. That's the context from which they interpret everything. And so you tell them something like that - there is nowhere to go and nothing to do and you can't do anything - and they say, "But I can. I can do things. Look, I can choose to punch you." Or, "I'm choosing to do this right now. I chose to come here. I chose to have this conversation with you, and I chose to give you a $20 donation for your meeting. So give me fucking enlightenment already."

This is what I've started to realize. Within the story there are two different orders of reality. And people are mixing them up. They're trying to use some concepts of the infinite in order to better their lives within this story. Because they think, "If I can just get this, then my life won't be so shitty anymore."

F: Yeah. That's the first thing we talked about. And honestly, you can't say that everybody has that idea, because while some people want to change a shitty situation, some people seek under the guise of wanting to be a teacher or a guru of some kind. Most people don't even think about enlightenment. Most of the time we're looking for something to change our current situation, as if the knowledge of enlightenment is going to change the fact that you still have responsibilities. You still have a life to live. You have a wife and kids or a husband. You still have things to do. None of this changes anything.

I fell into that kind of scenario. I got into sitting because something had to change. Then, as I read about all of the great and wonderful things that came along with enlightenment, I became more focused on how those cool attributes would just add to my personal movie.

J: Because the story is just a story. The story is always just a story. It's never going to be otherwise. There's no interaction between these orders. It's just that it's possible to discover that you are not what you've imagined yourself to be. And then, let the story go. Because then you realize that it's always been doing that anyway.

F: That's the kicker. Realizing that there's never been an individual you doing anything. Ever in your life. The good things and the bad things.

And you want to get rid of all the bad qualities and have just the good qualities. I want to understand how Joey understands it, but I don't want to be sick like he was. Someone wants to see things how I see them, but they don't want to have a breakdown and almost kill themselves with alcohol.

J: How are you going to get here from there anyway? Prepare yourself for a big shock. There's no way to bridge the gap. It's a complete break. Because there's no other way. We've talked about that too. You can't just shoot up heroin on the weekends.

F: Yeah. "I'll purposefully make myself an addict and go through withdrawal. Then I'll get it. Then I'll fool consciousness. I'll show you!"

Mystery and Collapse

I've heard some teachers insist that they are transmitting pure non-duality and other such nonsense. As far as I am concerned, statements like that are rubbish. Either that, or they are stating the obvious, which is what is already happening all the time. In which case, why mention it? Because then a steaming pile of dog shit is also transmitting pure non-duality. It's true. But it's misleading and not helpful.

So we're always left to hint at the obvious and utterly simple by means of the complex. We use words and metaphors and concepts to point to what is already here. We're just talking about what is unavoidable, what is all that is, what is this right now. Nothing complex. Just this. And yet, inevitably, we complicate it. And we approach it from one angle or another, which can give the false sense that reality as it is, is somehow knowable from a conceptual angle. Which is it is not.

In this conversation Fish and I talk about the mystery of true freedom, and we talk about exploring this mystery from different angles.

J: It is all a big mystery. Just reflecting back on this conversation so far, it's absolute nonsense. Everything that we say is absolute nonsense. It contradicts itself. And how do you communicate this clearly? It really is a puzzle, a mystery how to do that. How do you communicate it in a way that doesn't just sound like gibberish?

F: I think you're the first person that I've ever spoken to in depth with and not tried to get into some sort of competition. "My understanding is deeper than yours." Or that kind of thing. Sometimes when I talk to people it can get ugly pretty quickly. The conversation turns into a recital of verse and doctrine that leads nowhere.

When you don't get stuck in all of the dogma and bullshit, it's not so exciting.

You know there are some teachers who one decade will preach, "You already are that!" Then the following year, maybe fellowship is going down and donations aren't coming in. Now there's a new level to attain. You can come to the weekend class. Then you have to have level 2 and level 3 certifications. Then the one-on-one private session with the Roshi, just remember to exhale when you feel a little pressure.

So it is extremely difficult to communicate this with anybody. Even between you and me we still stumble over it. Because you can't describe this without contradicting yourself.

We're using words to describe it. Well, how else are we going to describe it? There are no real words that can describe this. But that's the difficulty that I think we have. And that's a massive, if not the biggest stumbling block: trying to describe it to someone else, if not ourselves.

J: As we're having this conversation, I'm realizing that inevitably you are never actually going to be talking directly of this. There's no way to do that. But you can talk around it. And you can come at it from all these different angles.

So from a certain perspective, as we talk about it, we talk about it as though there are two different orders of reality: the unbounded infinity of isness or even nothingness and then there's the story, as though they're two different things.

And we talk about there being the story or the story of me and my life, and the discovery is that I'm not that. But actually, then, the discovery is that you are that! That's what so puzzling about it.

Coming at it from that direction, what I've started to see is that as we conceive of ourselves, we then exclude aspects of the story. So we say, "I like winning the lottery, but I don't like cancer. And I don't like my girlfriend cheating on me. And all that stuff. Get rid of that. And use "The Secret" to win the lottery more and manifest parking spaces."

But then, what I'm seeing is that whole thing is duality right there. The notion that some things are included and others excluded. And I'm the one who is doing the including or excluding. So what I've started to point people to is to welcome it all. Allow all of it, especially whatever it is that you most want to avoid - let that one be here.

F: Yeah. We've talked about that one before. It doesn't matter if you let it be here or not. The suffering comes from when you don't want it to be here. But the universe doesn't need your permission.

J: That's true. And that's why I suggest to people that it's not like you're in charge here. It's not welcoming things because you get to choose what is here or not. It's just about aligning your perception with reality as it is. Just wake up and discover that this is already here. You can't get rid of it. You girlfriend's already cheated on you. That's already what's happening. All the wishing and praying and all the rest of that doesn't keep you safe.

But then it becomes more subtle. And that's what is challenging to point out to people. Notice every single strategy that you have for trying to avoid all this stuff that you don't like. And it just requires looking and noticing what you're doing right now to try to avoid what is here. Just seeing that can be very transformative because once you see it then you realize, "Oh shit! It won't work. It's totally not going to work! The way I hunch my shoulders is not going to protect me from this feeling."

F: Trying to avoid one and have the other one. It's just not going to work. We operate in a dualistic reality. To have one, you have to have the other to compare it to.

J: And then, when you finally discover that it's all already here anyway and that you don't choose it or control it in any way, then strangely - at least my experience is that even though on a certain level we can say that there are up and down, black and white, night and day - but actually it all collapses into just this. There is no way to separate it out any longer.

F: Yeah. That's the realization that it's all included in this. There are no parts to come back together. Even the notion that you feel that you're separate is that too. You're not looking in at totality. You're not merging back in with that. You already are that. You've never been apart from that. And that's the problem.

J: That's brilliant. You've nailed it. That's what I try to tell people. And why it gets confusing, I don't know. This is already it. You're never going to get something other than this because this is it.

F: You're already here.

J: The problem is that you think that you're the chooser, the thinker, the observer, the controller, the owner of all it. Actually, find it. Find that one. Because you can't. I promise you can't. And then, what you're left with is – ta-da! This is it. This is all that has ever been. And wow, in all it's horror and all it's glory, it's pretty fucking awesome.

F: It is. It is amazing. I'm not to the point where I'm running around singing and laughing all the time. I mean, I am laughing all the time but a lot of people misconstrue why I'm laughing. I just see the cosmic humor in it. And I know I said before that people don't talk to me because they're afraid that I'm going to laugh at them. But I'm not going to laugh at you maliciously. I just laugh because I see the futility of the search because I was adamant about the way I was going to do it. I was so hardcore. I thought I was this and I was that and everyone else was way off base. And now I just think what a fucking dumbass I was.

There's no other way to put it. I have no problem having a self-deprecating sense of humor about it. I know I offend other people with that. But from my way of looking at it, get as mad at me as you want. Just prove me wrong. I don't need you to read all kinds of books or anything. Just show me. Point me to the proof of your individual existence that isn't self-referencing. Go ahead. I'm waiting.

J: It's weird, isn't it? It's really interesting to me how there's this undeniable isness or presence or existence, aliveness, and that's fine. You can't deny it. It's here. It's what is. But somehow, we manage to twist that through this one really simple assumption into a whole big nightmare of me and my separate controlling life that I need to constantly maintain and protect and everything. And all you really need to do is simple, but I guess really not easy: just take a look and explore and see if you can find this thing that you've assumed to be true.

I don't come at it in that confrontational sort of way, but at the heart of it I say, "Prove that you exist as a separate self." And people tend to come back with "Well, I exist. That's the proof!" And I say, "Sure, yes. But prove that you exist separate from this."

You know, even the story exists. But there's no proof that it is separate from what is here. There is no separation that I can find.

F: There can't be. We think that words define us. And words are simply references to other things. And that's how we believe that we are. We believe that we're separate, but at the same time we reference other things around us. So it's almost like we have our own little duality.

But, I tell people, "Take it easy." But when you tell people to take it easy, they get fired up, saying, "It's easy for you to say!"

Well, actually, it is easy now that I realize that there never was a me to do anything. But like I said, I would have paid somebody to make me stop sitting and being as crazy as I was about this whole thing. There was no way I chose to do that. That was the first thing for me - there was no way that I purposefully chose to be this meditating, book-reading freak that was just sitting, spending all my time looking at the wall. I mean, who does that on purpose?

And then when you and I talk to people and say "Just stop and take a look," then that becomes a practice and they get hung up on that. But like we said before, some people want to be told, and you can't really tell people this. You can't just say, "Look, this is it right here!" And then they say, "I don't understand,"

J: Fish, I don't understand!

Being in Control

One of the most common conceptual stumbling blocks that I've noticed is this matter of no separate self and no control. We try to wrap our heads around that. And in the process, we come up with lots of counter arguments that we imagine are our evidence that we really are in control. For example, we imagine that if it seems as though we had a thought that we would turn left and then we turned left then that is proof of something. But actually, it's only proof that within the present story it seems as though that may have happened. That's it. It's not proof of control.

So the mistake is believing that something needs to change. As if the circumstances and appearances need to change in some way in order to demonstrate that you are not in control. Which they don't. Because actually, you've never been in control. Because actually, the you that you imagined could be in control is a fiction based on nothing more than an unexamined assumption.

Nothing needs to change. Nothing will change. Sure, appearance is always seemingly changing. But actually, nothing is happening.

Ah, the utter crap that we get to get away with when we talk about non-duality!

So in this conversation Fish and I talk about the illusion of control, the falling away of the illusion of control, and how you can tell if someone is really enlightened (you can't.) Oh, and then we get into the usual *pissing contest to see who is more enlightened. Once again, I pull the Nisargadatta trump card for the win.*

J: I used to want the secret wink or the tap on the forehead and then I'd "get it."

F: You wanted to get the Patriarch bowl and robe of Enlightenment?

J: But nobody can do it for you.

F: And you can't do it either.

J: You can't do it either.

F: I want to say that it's like an evolutionary thing that it's helpful to have the notion that we're actually in control, that we have free will, that if we do this then we get that. But it's hard to reconcile that and still function like a normal person and not walk around completely paralyzed by fear of being a deviant.

J: What's interesting to me is that in my experience not a lot has changed dramatically. The feelings and the perceptions remain pretty much the same. It's just that the interpretation has fallen away so the way in which I used to experience, in which it seemed as though I was doing everything, still is pretty much the same. But it's just that there was an interpretation before that I was doing all that stuff, and now the interpretation is not there. But what we could call the thoughts and the sensations and all that which I used to interpret as "I'm doing it" still happen.

F: There's no template. Someone could say, "Oh, there's still a sense of doership? Then you're not awakened." Or someone else could say, "You still have thoughts so you're obviously not awake." And then, "You're not the watcher so you're not awake." Or one of my favorites was something I heard the other day - "She's not abiding in the self." What the fuck is that?

J: People take this stuff so seriously. I mean, I used to. It seemed very serious. But now I realize there ain't nothing serious here at all. It's just happening! That's all. Why not? Why not all of it? Why not anything? Why not thoughts? Why not a sense of doership? Who gives a fuck?

F: The sense of doership, thoughts, and ego, all of it is part of it. Not even a part. It is it.

Like you said before, mountains are mountains, then they aren't mountains, and then now they are mountains.

I used to see the ego as a fictional character in my head, like an image of me in there somewhere. And I thought I would have to destroy the ego. And now it's like, yeah, there is the ego. But now my understanding is completely different than before. Because if there wasn't an ego then how would I respond to anything around me? I'd stick a spoon in my eye and be like, "I don't know what I am. I am all things."

J: Because it's all allowed. There's no reason to exclude any of it anymore because it doesn't matter. None of it has anything to do with you. It's not going to affect you in any way. I mean, you know that in the story of Fish, Fish was born, Fish has his life, and then Fish dies. And yeah, that's known. Okay. Wonderful!

F: That's great.

Except that I'll live forever because I got the special enlightenment. I mean, come on. I did eat the Osho O's cereal. So I got the certificate and immortality.

J: I'm more advanced than you. Because like Nisargadatta, I have no interest whatsoever in immortality.

F: You have the beard.

J: That's true, yeah.

F: I've just got the scruffy chin weasel, dammit!

The Look of Enlightenment

Let's face it - we have an idea of what true freedom looks like, and it usually doesn't look like this, whatever is here right now. Usually, we imagine that true freedom is something at least slightly exotic, as if we will get into some sort of special club and we'll learn the special look and the special posture and how to radiate that "enlightened energy."

At the very least we probably imagine that freedom will entail an absence of everything that we don't like.

All of which, of course, is the very obstacle to realizing the freedom that we already are.

Because true freedom doesn't have a particular look. True freedom looks like this, whatever this is right now. And that may be hard to believe, but it's true regardless of belief.

In this conversation Fish and I talk about the look of enlightenment as well as the worship of photos and finally the worship of the Avatar.

J: People have the weirdest ideas. They think that it's got to look a certain way. Like you've got to wear a loincloth and have your little ashram and just sit there in silence all day. And then you've definitely reached the fourth level of enlightenment. But why? What does that mean? It doesn't mean anything. There's nothing wrong with that, but it just doesn't happen to work out that way for everybody.

F: Especially here in the western world. That's just romanticizing another culture. In that culture maybe it's natural wear a loincloth or a robe or whatever. But we don't do that here. So if you realize that it's a cultural thing, that it doesn't mean anything, then it kind of takes away the power and the sensationalism. And then it doesn't sell.

Which is why I'm growing out the beard.

J: I had the beard long before. I had the beard when I was...

F: You were born with the beard.

J: Yeah. It was mostly because I got tired of shaving.

F: I got tired of shaving too. I let it grow out. But I have a whole head-sized cowlick. I can't even wax it into shape. It goes all sideways. It looks like I'm always riding a motorcycle. I don't think I could sell too many books like that.

I'll get to the books after I commission a painting of myself in a loincloth wrestling a lion. I'll send you a picture and you can worship that. But only if you sign up for a subscription. That's just the way to do it.

J: There's so much weird shit that goes on. It's bizarre. It's so puzzling to me. I've written about this. Why is it that people who otherwise seem very sensible and are authentic and have something genuine to offer - why is it they sell pictures of themselves for worship?

F: Because there's a need. As long as there's a seeker there'll be someone who will give you what you're looking for.

J: You can't get away from some of that on the part of the people who are seeking. They're coming with all the baggage of their ideas and concepts, and you can't fix all of that or set it all straight. But it just seems to me that there are certain things you can do that minimize things like that. For example, don't sell pictures of yourself for worship. Just as an idea.

F: I grew up in the old glam metal days. You could go buy whatever rock magazine was on the newsstand. And it would be like, "Yeah, man! There's Kiss and there's Cinderella and all the glam bands." And it's like, what's the difference between worshipping those guys and a guru? You know, posters up in your room; "Motley Crue Forever!"

You know, as a child people are like, "Well, he's just a kid." But an adult doing that? People are like, "Ummmm, he's kind of crazy."

I think the disingenuous part from some of these teachers is that they're enabling the seeker. It's just like sobriety with drugs and alcohol - you really don't want the person to stop seeking because they'll stop buying your books, and they'll stop coming to your ashram. And they're not going to pay $5000 to come see you in Maui. They're not going to support your crazy lifestyle.

So as long as you enable that, either in a subtle manner or in a really gross manner - you know, "I sweat in this shirt one day" - that market is going to exist. And that's what it is: a market.

I'd be more than happy to sell you one of my old, sweaty shirts. But nobody wants to wear it.

J: You can take it to the extreme like Adi Da who said, "Worship me as God. I am God."

F: No thanks. That's just a little ridiculous.

Practice

Normally we imagine that there's something we must be able to do in order to attain what we most desire. And this assumption is the source of much suffering. Because we fail to see that any practice to produce some change presumes that there is someone separate and something else other than this - neither of which is true, and both of which form the foundation of suffering.

So in this conversation Fish and I explore - the whole notion of practice. We look at how practice is essentially an obstacle, and how the "practice" of letting go of all our practices of avoidance and pursuit may point you to what you've never been able to avoid anyway. Which is yourself as you are. Which is freedom.

F: When you and I talk about this stuff I think about how the conversations are going to be pretty cool and interesting. And it's exciting and I tell other people about it, and they say, "What's it going to be about?" And I say, "Nothing, really." For a lot of us, everything has to have a reason and some kind of endgame or goal. And they want to know why we're going to do it. And I say, "I don't know. Why not?"

Or sometimes people will say, "Are you going to be prescribing a practice?" And I say, "No. Not really. Maybe just investigation."

J: I'd look at it like there is a practice that you do already. So the "practice" that I would give to somebody is to stop doing your practice. So you have to become aware of what your habitual practice is. Which is assuming that you are who you think you are and are acting accordingly and trying to avoid yourself and all the things that you don't like. And that is what hasn't worked out so well. So take a look, see what you do and be willing not to do that any longer. And that usually is terrifying. Because then you're going to die.

F: Because that's your identity. And any practice, whether it's identifying with victim, hero, loser, winner - any threat to that is terrifying. Whatever it is. It could be being a drunk or being sober. That could be just downright horrifying for people. It's no wonder people cling to the fantastic version of understanding without seriously considering that everything is going to shatter. You know that, right?

J: That would be a good book - Everything's Going to Shatter, You Know That Right? You thought it was all going to be better, but actually it's going to be worse. It's going to be a lot worse. But, the good news is that it's much more restful this way.

F: It is. And what I'm grateful for is the peace that comes with it. Before I would have said, "I've got to do that to get that? Forget it. I'll figure something else out. I'll do something else." Because this wouldn't have intrigued me. If someone would have said, "Fish, you're going to be alright. Just relax. Everything is going to be okay. You're going to be at peace."

Well, I didn't want to be at peace. I was a fighter. I was aggressive and yelling and screaming all the time. I was okay with that. Or so I told myself. But, again, that doesn't sell books or t-shirts.

J: Personally, I was plenty angry and plenty violent. But never overtly. That wasn't how I conceived of myself. But I still had the idea that "I don't want peace. That sounds pretty dull. I mean, sure, I want peace in the sense of an escape from all my problems. But that's where I draw the line. Then, I want really good stuff. I want supreme knowledge and understanding and power. And I want to levitate and be able to do stuff like that." I mean, not that I would admit that openly. But secretly, in the back of my mind that's what I wanted.

F: Of course now you can. Like we can make fun of ourselves for believing in Santa Claus as kids.

But again, that's part of the story, which is part of this. There's no good and no bad. So a lot of people - that's their strife - they don't want to admit that to themselves. They don't want to be uncomfortable. They imagine that they want to be all loving and a healer. They want the cool things without looking at the bad things.

J: When you put it like that, it becomes so obvious. Like somebody has that idea that they want to be a healer. But think about that for just a moment, even just logically, what is implicit in that is that there needs to be a whole lot of fucked up stuff that needs to be healed. Otherwise you can't be a healer. Healer requires the fucked up stuff. So just recognize that and... But then maybe you say, "Well, yeah, but I want the fucked up stuff to be over there, away from me."

F: Yeah. I don't want to get dropped in the middle of somewhere where people actually suffer.

It's crazy because you want to be a hero. I mean, you don't really want things to be messed up most of the time, but that's what's implicit in your desires. I think admitting that you want to be a hero or savior is a huge step. Just admitting it to yourself. You don't have to run around the world admitting it. I'm not a fan of shishkabobing yourself. "I've got all these fantasies!" But just admitting it to yourself is a huge step.

J: The things that pop into my mind when you say, "I've got all these fantasies" are disturbing.

F: Let's keep that for another conversation.

J: Finally, that really is the freedom - complete willingness for it to be as it is. Because it is that way anyway.

F: And to belabor the point, this doesn't need your permission to be this. Realizing that you don't have any say in it anyway. So what are you agreeing to anyway? Because nothing needs you to say, "Okay, this can happen." That's not how it works.

J: It's just sanity. That's all.

F: In worrying about how things should be and how you want them to be and why they're this way, you can't have that peace, which is at the bottom of it all. It will elude you forever.

J: It's very confusing to talk about because I know what the concerns are that come up for people around this. "If I'm sick should I just not do anything? Do I not go to the store and get food anymore? Do I not get out of bed?"

Well, okay. Good luck with that. See if that works out for you. I don't think it will.

If you just want to play in the realm of what if and maybe and fantasy and thinking about it and all future projection, then you can do that forever. But if you're willing to actually just test it out, then just see what happens. Don't pursue anything any longer, and don't reject anything any longer. And just find out what happens. Because I'm pretty sure that you'll find that it happens exactly as it always has.

F: Yeah. That's exactly it. You didn't make the decision to go to the store in the first place. You didn't make the decision to go to work in the first place. Decisions were just made. And then the little inkling came in after that, "I did that." Once you realize that it's been bullshit the entire time, then if the option is to lie around, then lay around. Because guess what? Nobody cares. I mean, maybe your family would care. But you're just going to keep doing the same things you've been doing.

J: Yeah. For the most part. Again, it's confusing. This realization doesn't change your life in any way. And yet, it does, in a strange way. Because it might. You might stop doing the really stupid shit that you never really wanted to do anyway.

F: It might stop you from alienating everyone around you because you can't have a normal conversation without interjecting some Sanskrit bullshit. Trying to put in a snippet from the Dhammapada everywhere.

J: "Well, Ramana said..."

F: Yeah. You say things like "Well, Sri Babakanoosh said..."

And your wife says "Uh, Fish, that doesn't really apply. We're having dinner."

And of course being the non-duality police that you are you say "Oh yeah? Well, who's having dinner?" and then sit back in your asshole robe and wonder why you have no friends.

J: "You're not abiding in the self, goddammit!"

F: "You're not eating the celery in the self, loser."

"What do you mean you're sitting in a chair watching TV? I'm in half lotus. I'm so much more advanced than you."

If I had a time machine I'd go back in time and slap myself. Multiple times.

That could be the topic for another conversation: how to be a genuine douche bag.

Self-Censorship and Deceit

At the end of our third conversation Fish and I started talking about practical matters - what would happen next and who would do what. And strangely, this part of the conversation reveals some important things - honesty and vulnerability - that I think may be helpful for some readers. And so I'm including this part of the conversation here.

What I like about this exchange is that we reveal elements of our humanness without distracting from the subject of the book.

F: So now that we've more or less wrapped up this conversation, what do we do now? You'll transcribe it and then what?

J: Yeah, I'll transcribe it, compile everything and put it together in document that you can review and make whatever edits you want.

F: Well, I don't really want to go back and sanitize any of it.

J: Well, if you think that you can improve or clarify any of it then go for it. But yeah, let's keep it authentic and real. I'm not suggesting that you should sanitize it.

F: You know, back in the military everyone used to say, "Damn, Fish. You said it exactly how we wanted to say it, but we didn't want to say it." And that's why I was the low man on the ranking totem pole. Because I was a loud mouth jackass. "Thanks for having my back, bitches!"

And with this kind of stuff, I can't be the only one who feels this way. Just tired of the fucking bullshit, and looking for someone who says, "Fuck it." Yeah, I said, "Fuck." I said, "Shit." I cuss like a sailor because I was one. There's nothing wrong with that. And I think some people will find that refreshing.

J: Absolutely. The published version of this should have the spontaneity and freshness just like these conversations.

You know, normally, when I write I tend be a little more on the conservative side. Even though I tell it like it is and I don't have any problem calling bullshit bullshit. But in terms of language, I do tend to keep it kind of clean. It's not a censorship issue. That's just what happens. But these conversations are authentic in the sense that it's how I tend to speak. And I agree with you that there's something refreshing about a book on this subject that is a little freer in the ways in which we speak about these things. Because truth includes it all.

So I've got this book that I'm about to publish through Non-Duality Press. They've got it for editing right now. And there's a whole chapter in there where I talk about my Derrick Jensen phase. Derrick Jensen is a radical leftist environmentalist. He advocates for all the hippie tree-sitters to get out of the trees and get some explosives and blow shit up. So there was a period in my life during which that seemed like the only thing that could give me meaning. I felt that I needed meaning. Everything was fucked. And this seemed like the answer. So I write about that in the book.

And then I have a doubt - do I really want to put that out there? Because that's going to turn some people off. It's possibly distracting. But then I realize that it's authentic.

That really did happen. And I know that there's got to be people out there where that will help them. They'll say, "Somebody else is dealing with this." Maybe not the specifics, but the deep angst and suffering and hopelessness and pointlessness and meaninglessness of it all. And here's a message that might click for them.

F: Sure. Or maybe some people have guilt that they even had those thoughts or feelings. Or, like me, they cuss too much and look at porn. And so someone can tell you, "Hey, I do that too, and it doesn't change anything."

Personally, I wanted to be a SEAL when I first joined the Navy. I didn't know anything about glamour and movies and shit like that back then. I wanted to fucking kill people. I wanted to kill the bad guys.

J: You wanted to kill the eco-terrorists.

F: And when we went over to the Gulf the first time it was when divers had slashed some Greenpeace boats. I went over there, and sure enough, there was a Greenpeace boat parked in front of ours. So I went down there, and I was like, "Ha ha, faggots! Navy divers, that's us, we cut your fucking boats."

The guy on the boat looked at me and said, "Well, actually, we're here to protect the environment. Not just the U.S. government, but everyone is destroying everything over here." I was like, "You're full of shit." And then I got in the water, and wow, there was unprocessed human feces and dead fish and it was just horrific. I thought to myself, "Damn. Don't I feel like an asshole?"

J: That's interesting. I never really thought about that, but as a diver, you're probably rather sensitive to the conditions of the oceans.

F: I am. I see just how destructive man is and it saddens me.

It's funny how your beliefs, the ones that you absolutely know are true, change over time. I used to want to kill bad guys overseas. And now that I'm older, I realize that if I had to go past a checkpoint every day, I'd be a little pissed off too. If I was an Afghani, I'd be a little angry with the U.S. government. So I have sympathy. I watched Red Dawn. Wolverines!

You realize that your idea of the bad guy is determined by what you read or hear or whatever. The people in other countries are fed some kind of truth, just like we are. I've worked with Special Forces and have watched my friends go into the shit. While we praise them as heroes, the people on the other side see them as killers.

J: And you also start to see that it's all the way that you try to protect yourself. You try to build up this whole identity that you think it going to keep you safe, and then finally you realize that it's not going to work.

F: Who knows what would have happened had I made it into Special Forces? I can't imagine a different life than the one I have now and I realize that everything that has happened in my life has led up to now - Shazam! - Hey, I need to get a little gong that I can carry around with me.

J: Yeah, I can introduce the book version of these conversations saying that these conversations were very challenging because Fish kept banging that fucking gong. So I'm not sure that I got it all transcribed correctly.

F: Every few sentences Fish bangs the gong, waiting for acknowledgement. [Gong sound] "Yes, Fish."

J: "Fish, you're a genius"

F: [Gong sound]

J: "Fish, you're brilliant."

F: That's how I roll.

Is Enlightenment An Escape?

The phenomenon of seeking is synonymous with suffering. And we tend to seek in different guises for much of our lifetime. We seek for money, love, security, health and perhaps "spirituality."

The nature of seeking is that we are looking toward something, pursuing something. So we don't often notice that seeking is actually the positive polarity of a duality. The negative polarity is the thing that we fear - that which we wish to escape.

The myth of enlightenment is a fantasy that we concoct to create yet another positive polarity to chase after as a way to attempt to escape the fear. But most of us don't see that. We wrongly imagine that we are engaged in a noble (i.e. better than the profane) pursuit toward a lofty and valuable goal, when in fact we are trying to escape from ourselves, which is the source of suffering.

This conversation began with the question, "Is enlightenment an escape?"

J: That sure is what we want it to be.

F: We're not looking for something when times are good. We look at this just like any other form of escape. Like being a World of Warcraft warrior or drinking or drugs, you want to get away from whatever moment you're in. You want to get away from here.

J: I think that's what we're always doing. Enlightenment is just another concept that's the same thing, just a different disguise. Because that's what we've always been doing from the moment we started trying to escape. "I'm going to become a doctor or an astronaut." Not that there's anything wrong with those ambitions, but we can turn them into an attempt to escape. And then at some point we get disillusioned with what we were doing. You know, maybe we didn't make the cut for astronaut training, so then we look for another attempt to escape. And after a decade of drinking didn't work out, then we read a book by so-and-so. So now we're going to get enlightened in order to escape the horrors of our lives.

It's hard to communicate that, though. Because you can say that. I've said that many times. And then people say, "Right. I understand that. But how do I escape? How do I get rid of all this stuff that I don't like?"

F: Right. You want to get rid of the bad things and keep the good things. That's the whole escape part of this whole enlightenment thing. You want to get away from this and all these troubles that you're having. But you're the center of your problems. Wherever you go things are going to happen and they're going to revolve around you or whatever story you've got. So where else are you going to go?

But you can't really tell people that because we're conditioned to constantly be seeking, striving and setting goals. Otherwise we're seen as lazy. It just doesn't jibe with our sense of becoming. We can't focus on being because we're too busy focusing on becoming something else.

J: That's true. I also think a big part of it is a primal fear. We're usually so busy that we don't notice it. But when we finally can't attempt to avoid it, then we realize that what we've been running from is this primal fear.

I'm curious, was that your experience?

F: I was an alpha male. For me there was a huge trust issue. That was what was holding me back. In the military you had to put your life in somebody else's hands. Literally, you had to trust somebody else to do his job so that you didn't die. So trust was a huge issue. And if you didn't trust yourself - something was wrong. Some people look at military personnel and say that they're just arrogant bastards. But no, they're just confident. They have to be. If they're not, then they have to find another job. Because then that lack of trust in themselves is going to get people killed.

So with seeking, because I didn't have a teacher or guru, I was trusting myself that I could get this. But the realization that there was nothing at all that I could do to get this was terrifying. That was the scariest part for me. You've got to let go. You've got to trust that it's going to be okay. You have to trust that things are going to be fine just as they are.

Sometimes, because of that lack of trust, you'll throw up roadblocks to this understanding. And you can't just say that you'll trust when you've got that little disclaimer that says, "Yeah, but I'm still here in case things don't go right. In case this doesn't work out I'll take over the reins."

When people say, "I'm going to sit back and let God take the reins on this one," I'm like, "Really? I didn't know you were that powerful that you were wrestling this from the almighty."

J: That's the arrogance.

F: Yeah. It's an arrogance mixed in with the fear that you can't face the unknown because it is the unknown and you're not really sure. And we convince ourselves that we can handle whatever comes up. We're so smart and we're so tough and this and that. And I think that's part of why we start seeking in the first place, because there are things that come up that we just can't handle. The reality of what is going on.

The illusion of awakening is that all those things will go away. You can build this fantasy about what this is going to be, but in reality it's an even greater unknown. It's beyond your comprehension. It's not even close. You can stop drinking or other habits. Those things seem to be under your control, even though they're not. But this is beyond any semblance of control you'll ever have.

There's no way you can wrap your hands around it. Which was my downfall. I couldn't choke it into submission. I couldn't wrestle it down and hold it and say, "I own you." It was something completely foreign to me, which completely terrified me.

J: So we get into this whole mess hoping that it will be an escape. And then eventually we realize that it won't be an escape. But then by that point maybe we're in too deep. At least in my experience, I knew too much, I had seen too much and I was so miserable that I couldn't stop. It seems to me that the more I searched the more miserable I became. But I couldn't go back. I knew it wasn't an escape, but there was no other opportunity.

F: It's like a bad car wreck. You can't undo it. You can't forget what you saw.

I was on the seeking train and wondering how the hell I was going to get off it. The illusion is that the more you learn, the more habits you pick up and the more rituals you add on to your story, the deeper your understanding is going to be and the easier it will be to escape from whatever it is that you're trying to escape from. But that's not the case. All you've done is put more icing on that shit sandwich.

J: Yeah. Or, more shit on the shit sandwich. That was my experience. Like you talked about. Sitting for you became an addiction. If you couldn't sit at the right time and in the right place then your day was ruined. And it's like that. You start to realize that all the stuff that you're doing to try and escape from the suffering is just creating the suffering for you.

F: It's just become another avenue for you to suffer more.

Trust the Guru

In my (probably not so) humble opinion, the days of the gurus have passed. We don't need no stinkin' gurus! (Yes, I did just reference a Weird Al movie.) While the guru-disciple relationship in the conventional sense may have served a valuable purpose for many, our cynicism has grown too thick and choked out the possibilities of true guru-disciple relationships for most of us.

So what is the alternative? What is the role of trust?

In this conversation Fish and I explore this subject. We begin with a question, "What is the importance of trust in the guru?"

J: It's interesting. I'm pretty sure that I'm anti-guru. I don't think that whole guru game is helpful. Maybe at a different time and in a different culture it would be very helpful. But I don't think that at this time and in this culture it's helpful. Because there's just too much opportunity for abuse.

I think what we really need are honest people who can be guides. And then trusting the guide is important. For example, are you going to go on some sort of jungle trip with a guide you don't trust? One who will leave you stranded to get eaten by a snake? No! You have to trust.

F: You're right that there's a lot of opportunity for abuse and egotism. "I am God. Listen to me." And I think it's such a rarity that you have someone who is sincere in the message that they are trying to get across and you have the sincerity of the seeker.

The responsibility is on both parties. If someone schedules a meeting with you and then just tells you how they think it is, going on a diatribe about how it really is, why did they call you in the first place? What's the point of reading the book or going to a meeting then?

J: Yeah. Just have your own meeting.

F: "Yeah. Go start your own ashram, loser! These are my dirty bums!"

J: We have lots of ideas. There are rules. If you're going to be a "spiritual teacher" then there are rules - a social contract. And I think that's not helpful either.

So I have people tell me that they see me as a teacher. And I suggest that they see differently because that's part of the obstacle. Because I'm not. Ask my kids if I'm a spiritual teacher. And they will tell you no.

Getting rid of those sorts of things can be helpful. And then breaking the expected contracts can also be helpful. For example, if someone comes and just wants to be argumentative, then just say, "Get the fuck out of here." And people may gasp and say, "Oh my god. You can't say that. It's not spiritual." Well, so this is a perfect opportunity to explore what exactly is spiritual? Because it's just a made up, bullshit concept. It's just a way of constraining behavior so that it makes people comfortable. They can believe that since they're going to a "spiritual" meeting then they can have "spiritual" experiences. And that is what keeps you stuck in a conceptual safety zone, which is miserable. So let's break that.

F: Like you can't see this without a guide.

When I used to run my classes, I would say, I'm not giving you anything. I'm just showing you what you have already. And for a lot of people once they saw that - like doing a pull-up - my job was done.

So the sincerity of the teacher is to just point to what you've already got. I don't know about the mind-to-mind transmission or the passing of the flame from one to the other. It's just the belief in the teacher.

If someone comes to me then I just point him or her in a direction. I can't hold their hand because it doesn't work like that.

Disillusion

Ironically, the belief that we can achieve freedom is often one of the biggest obstacles to realizing freedom. So disillusion is often necessary. Disillusion is different than cynicism because it is the disappearance of or transparency of belief without replacement. In cases of cynicism one belief is replaced with another, harder belief. Disillusion is the end or transparency of belief that leaves only openness in its place.

Disillusion, of course, is not strictly synonymous with the discovery of freedom. Because disillusion may not be the complete transparency of all things. It may only be the transparency of some things. So when disillusion appears then the opportunity, as always, is to examine any remaining assumptions and let it all go.

In this conversation we begin with the question that Fish poses: how to go guru-less? And then we look at disillusion. And finally, we talk about the dropping of everything and the discovery of essential nothingness. Fun stuff.

J: It's rare, I guess, that somebody can see what we're pointing to completely on his or her own. It seems that it does happen. But it seems that it's more common when it happens in the context of a relationship with someone who has already seen. So that can be helpful and potentially very valuable when you find the right person who you can trust and who can just be a guide instead of trying to be your guru.

I'd say that even if you're just reading a book then the book is serving as that guide, and it's just pointing repeatedly to what you've been trying to avoid. We're so in the habit of looking everywhere else that finally that's it. Just looking in the one place that you haven't been looking. So having someone who can point you to that over and over and over again can be useful. And in the absence of that, having the persistence within yourself to keep looking to what you've been avoiding is what is needed.

F: And I think it goes back to identification. For some people, when they get involved in this, then their identity is that of a seeker. And if they find the understanding...for some people you have to wonder if they ever want to stop seeking. They don't want to stop, and anything that threatens that...For a lot of people being a seeker is as good as anything else.

J: I think it depends on how intense the suffering is, because anything can serve that role. As long as the suffering isn't intense enough, then it's just another thing. It's just more entertainment.

F: Monday morning meditation.

J: Yeah. But once the suffering is great enough then I think that you get more honest about it. "I really don't want to keep seeking. But I'm confused about what to do. I used to think I knew what I was doing. I used to think that I was taking steps in the direction of enlightenment." And then you get to a point where the suffering is great enough and you realize, "I don't know what I'm doing any longer. I don't even know what this seeking thing is meant to arrive at. I don't even know what I'm seeking for anymore." And that's a very important point because then you can start to take a look at why you're seeking. And from my perspective seeking will never get you anywhere because the seeking is just the attempt to escape from something. If seeking can ever point to something, it's only in the end of the seeking that you realize the seeking was just another strategy to try and avoid this that you are.

F: Once there's nothing to seek and you're no longer a seeker, then what?

J: I guess at that point you could still keep seeking in a different guise. Or, you could finally just drop the whole thing.

F: Yeah. In my experience the neurotic seeking energy isn't present anymore. Thankfully. And it's just like any other form of identification, as much as it seemed like it was good for you at the time. Once it's gone, you're like, "Wow, man, thank god! Thank god that shit's over."

J: Yeah. It's strange. We start these things and at first we have all this hope and expectation that this is going to be it. Like I finally got the right job, I'm going to make a bunch of money and all my problems are going to go away. And then after awhile you realize that you're working 60-70 hour weeks. You're miserable. And so you quit, and you're like, "Wow. This is so much better."

F: "What a relief! I'm back to where I was before I had the job. Goddammit!"

J: That is the obstacle. I've seen this with seeking identification. With the seeking you really are building yourself up to be some sort of special person. Like you're getting closer and closer to this special thing called enlightenment. And then to give that up means, like you just said, you're back to square one. You are nothing and no one. And that's what you've been trying to escape.

F: You built up an image. Before you learned about spirituality you didn't know. And then you learned about it and you knew. And you created this whole miserable world for yourself that you need to escape from. And all of a sudden, the understanding comes, and you're like, "Wait a second! I'm back to where I was before I started reading all this bullshit!"

J: That's why when I talk to people and they want me to make them better, I say, "Well, sorry, I can't do that. I can only do the opposite of that."

F: "I can relieve you of the stress of having money. Give it all to me now."

Maturity of the Seeker

Of course, nothing that I could ever write is strictly true. All that I can do is point and then make observations about generalities, which may be helpful. For example, in the previous section we spoke about disillusionment, which is something that can happen seemingly to some seekers. But it may not always seem to happen. That's just the nature of appearance - it is totally unpredictable and meaningless.

Similarly, in the case of the conversation that follows, it is not strictly necessary that there be a maturity on the part of the seeker in order to discover what already is. Because ultimately this discovery is not made by the seeker. The discovery is the end of or the transparency of the seeker. So there are absolutely no requirements placed upon the seeker to awaken. The apparent seeker could be drunk in the gutter or meditating in a cave at the seeming moment of discovery. Because the discovery really is timeless and it doesn't even actually happen. It is the discovery that nothing can happen.

Still, there does appear to be a phenomenon whereby a certain maturation is possible within the seeker. And by maturation, what I probably really mean is just a climax of suffering. The subjective experience of that suffering or maturation will always be different, of course. But there may come a point where the seeker ceases to believe that escape is possible. And at this point the seeker may finally be open to the invitation to discover what is already here.

J: You said something, which I think is important. Having the right guide and the right seeker is important. Somebody has to be mature in their seeking, so to speak. Because otherwise, if you're not, then if you come to somebody who says, "What I can offer you is to take away everything, leave you with nothing, and you're just going to be left with everything that you've tried to escape from. How does that sound?" And most people would say, "Uh, no thank you. Get me out of here."

F: "I'm going to go to the other guy."

J: Exactly. "I'm going to go to the guy who can tap me on the forehead and give me siddhis and all that stuff." But for most people who consider themselves sane - like people who are not even seekers - and they heard somebody say something like that, you know, like, "I'm going to take away everything, strip away all of you progress and leave you naked, bare, in the gutter with all your shit." They'd think that sounds absolutely insane. Who on earth would want that? But then the person comes along who has been seeking and suffering miserably, and they say, "Yes! Thank god! That's what I want."

F: "Yes. Please. Leave me stripped bare to the bone."

And that has to be a willingness on the seeker's part.

For me, I wasn't trying to let go of all this stuff. I was trying to become the supreme guru. I wanted all this crazy cool stuff. And then for me it was all just stripped away. There was no willingness or surrender.

From my standpoint, I was in amazing shape, I was strong, I ran a popular class, I was super healthy. People looked at me like, "Fish, what are you trying to get away from?" And I was like, "I don't know. All I know is something's not right here. And I don't even know what I'm looking for," But it all just got stripped away. There was no willing surrender. I think there comes a point where, like you've said before, you're just exhausted. Then there's no other option.

J: Yeah. I don't think you can do it willingly. But I think a lot of people already are past that point. They have suffered enough, but they just keep going on caffeine and amphetamines or something. So then there's an opportunity when they can speak with someone who understands and can invite them to discover that they already are stripped bare. There's never been anything there.

Whereas, most people, most of the time, aren't able to receive that opportunity.

What Do You Want to Escape From?

Part of the apparent maturation may be the realization that we've been lying to ourselves all along. We imagined that we were pursuing something noble and great. But once we cease to be able to believe in those fantasies, we are left with what we've been running from. So we realize that we were trying to escape all along.

In this conversation we discuss this phenomenon of trying to escape, specifically exploring Fish's experiences.

J: You brought up an interesting point. You said that you don't know what you were trying to escape from. But do you now have any insights into that?

F: Looking back, even though from an outside perspective, granted, I didn't have a lot of money or stuff. I was just a kid. I had a, "I don't give a shit" attitude. I knew deep down that the image that I had of myself wasn't me. There was a little bit of trying to figure out who I really was. I could see the cartoon image I had of myself. Am I a fighter? Am I a diver? Am I this ex-military guy? Am I this trainer? Am I this coach? Am I this boyfriend, husband, friend? What am I?

I looked at this thing, and I already understood that I was looking at an image or thought process. So what is the thing that's looking? I didn't understand how to do that. I had an idea. I had been in the zone with sports or fighting.

So I wanted to be in that state all the time. But I knew that being Fish - as great as it seemed to be - ultimately wasn't me.

I'm not going to romanticize that ever since I was a child I wondered, "Who am I?"

"Really?"

"No."

J: I was the Dalai Lama in a past life.

F: Really? I thought I was.

For me there was an uneasiness with the facade. I could be all these great things, but at the same time I was sometimes insecure and very introverted when by all accounts I should have been anything but. So I was like, "Okay. What is happening here?" There was a strange sense that if I'm not this then what am I? There was a general unease in my own skin that I wasn't familiar with. I'd read all the sports psychology and motivational books, and none of it was working. I convinced myself of these things, and I was like, "Goddamn, what is going on here?"

I've met a lot of people like that, too. They don't know what it is that they're trying to get away from. I would ask people, "What are you drinking for? What are you looking for?" I remember I went to this guy's house with my girlfriend's mother. She was a seeker. There was a bunch of people sitting around. And I was like, "What are you guys looking for?" You know, I didn't know what it was, but I was angry that they didn't know either. I was like, "What is driving you to not get up in the morning and figure this stuff out?" They gave me some weird explanation and I was like, "Are you high? Who talks like that?" I felt that there had to be an endgame here. But I didn't know what it was. I didn't know what I was looking for.

J: So did you find the endgame?

F: There is no endgame.

J: So it sounds like you were looking. You could see everything that you are not. You wanted to know who are you.

F: Yeah. People have asked me about this, "So did you find out who you are?" And I say, "I found out what I'm not."

J: That was basically what I was curious to know.

F: Oh, you were testing me?

J: It's important. We've got to know what level you're on.

F: I haven't done the one-on-one with my guru in the birthday suit yet.

The endgame is there is no endgame. You create the bad situation. Then you create the convoluted way to become free of the bad situation that you created. And you convince yourself that you can't do it unless somebody else tells you that you can, which is probably not a formula that I'm going to put into future books. Because that would probably prevent sales.

J: So you think that it's fair to say that the problem isn't really so much who are you, but trying to be someone?

F: Yeah.

Masks and Stories

Most of us go through life imagining that we are something. Rarely do we even notice that the thing that we imagine ourselves to be is itself fluid - constantly changing. There isn't actually a thing there at all!

The discovery that what you have imagined yourself to be is nothing more than a fantasy - a conceptualization of an ever-changing, fluid, transient apparent movement - can be simultaneously liberating and terrifying. The liberation is the discovery that you have never done anything and neither can you do anything - that, in fact, you are nothing. The terror is in still subtly identifying as something separate.

My best advice is to see that true freedom is not a static thing. True freedom is not a realization or an experience. It is an endless reception of yourself as you are, which includes all appearance. So whatever happens, the invitation is to receive it as yourself. Simply stop, let go, fall and dissolve, discovering anew that stopping, letting go, falling and dissolving are always already the case. You cannot do any of it. Nothing is even happening. There is no possibility of clinging, so welcome even the appearance of clinging as yourself.

F: You have the concocted story of who you are. Then someone tells you that you're not that story. So then you struggle to put together a better story, which includes the chapter on enlightenment. You don't want to be that guy who's been a disaster his whole life. Now you want to be the spiritual guy who is awakened.

It's not that the illusion of who you are is the problem. It's believing the illusion that is the problem. I mean, you can pretend things all day long. We're different people to others all the time. I mean, you talk to your kids differently than you talk to me. At least I hope so.

J: Not really! That's why they cry so much.

F: That's why they're traumatized?

We put on different masks all the time. I mean, that's society. It's just when you take any one of those masks and you believe that it's really real. That's when the problem starts. It doesn't matter what the mask is. Seeing through the illusion of the masks finally sets you free. Then you can play any of those roles fully. Because it's not life and death to protect them. Then you're carefree.

J: I also think that it's seeing that none of those things actually exists. We conceptualize that if we are a certain way with our kids then that is a thing. But actually, there is no such thing. If you tell the truth, then every moment is completely spontaneous. It's completely different.

F: When I started getting into some books I started to wonder when does this moment stop and the next one begin? Then I drove myself nuts for a while trying to see when this moment became the next one.

J: Yeah. You just start to take a look at all these assumptions. In our language we talk about all these things. Which is fine. But like you said, when you take it seriously and believe that it's real then you're just going to be really confused and frustrated. Because at heart, you know that none of it is real. None of it exists. It is just fantasy.

Like you said. We talk about moments. But where is a moment? Where is the dividing line between two moments?

And then you start to see that the concept of yourself is exactly the same way. Because there's nothing there. It's just constant movement.

F: Yeah. It's a flowing.

I heard about marriage described as a lifetime of portraits strung together to make a mosaic.

And that's kind of how your life is. It's just snapshots that you remember selectively - good or bad depending on how you feel - and you string them together to make a movie about yourself. That's always changing. It's not a solid thing. It's a flowing process.

I think that for a lot of people, if you see that your fundamental beliefs about yourself change over time and that you can change your memories or just different aspects of your memories to help you deal with the past better - like they do in some types of therapy - then what is real? If I can change my entire childhood just by changing a color of the memory or the way people talked, then what really happened?

J: The interesting thing is that when you follow that to its natural conclusion it can be either extraordinarily liberating or send you into madness. Because if there's nothing that is real, but you still cling to the notion that there is a separate self, then it's like, "Wow! I'm all alone in this complete nothingness universe!" That can be terrifying.

F: For me, I was devastated.

Transition

I have heard many speak in various ways of a period of transition between the discovery of no separation and what I can only term the maturation of this discovery. Others speak of this as stabilization or they may use other terms. Frankly, words completely fail to describe what absolutely doesn't happen.

I'm sorry that I cannot speak with any more clarity on this subject. I think the point here is truly that what is happening in this transition is the complete dissolution of any delusion that anything has ever happened. And so to speak of it coherently is impossible. Because we're talking about something that happens that reveals that nothing has ever happened.

For some apparent people this apparent transition is apparently quite smooth. In my own experience, it seems that the discovery of no separation to a maturation of comfort in discomfort was smooth. We could theorize that this is because in my own case there was such intensity of suffering, misery and dissolution prior to the epiphany. Of course, that is just a story so it's totally meaningless. And it does no good for anyone because what appears to have been my experience isn't likely to be anyone else's experience.

Case in point: Fish had a sudden epiphany - a falling away of a sense of self - and then that was followed by a decade of very difficult transition. Of course, others will argue that this is not true. And that's *fine. Because it's not true. It's just a story. But as far as it goes, this story is pretty good. So I'll go with it for now.*

The question we explore in this conversation is, is there anything that could or should be done to support someone in this transition? I argue that there is and that whenever possible we ought to offer that support. Of course, the support can only come from one who knows nothing except that he or she is nothing. Which is to say, the support can only come from nothing. And in the absence of an apparent person to offer live support, a book may do.

Here's my advice: if you find yourself in this transition and you are struggling, then stop. Let go. Question the assumptions. Your conceptualization of what has happened will always be wrong. So let it all go. Drop everything. There is no point of arrival. There is only the falling.

And if you need support, then find it. Send me an email.

J: As far as the story goes, if there's any purpose or value in something like Zen, it's really just to prepare you, to give you the understanding, so that when it all falls away and you're left with nothing, at least then you realize, "Oh, this is it! This is what they've been talking about." But for you, it sounds like, that didn't really help.

F: Zen prepares you to put Zen away. When this finally happens then you put Zen away. But just like any other way of coming about this, it really can't prepare you. I can't say that while I was sitting, insights didn't happen that normally wouldn't have happened. Because I was reading and contemplating and things would come up. But for me, I had absolutely no idea. I read things I wanted to agree with. The perfection. The light. The flowing things. I brought my own baggage filled with ideas on how I thought it was supposed to be, to every book that I read.

J: So you didn't get a lot of the emptiness, nothingness teaching?

F: No. I didn't understand what that meant. "What are you talking about, nothing?"

And then, "Oh! That's what you're talking about! That's absolutely terrifying. I think I'm going to drink myself to death!"

There's really nothing that can prepare you. In the context of Zen, I had a kensho moment. And everybody's experience is different. For some people it's like, "I was just walking along and then I realized." And then for other people it's very traumatic with confusion and crying. And I went through that. I was just bawling my eyes out. I was afraid. I had no idea.

J: In a case like that, I guess that if you're lucky enough, having a guide could be helpful. I think it's really about reorienting to all of it. Because really, what has changed? Nothing.

F: Nothing. Nothing has changed but my view on everything did.

J: But somehow, what it seemed you had to get away from no matter what, all of a sudden collapsed into nothingness, which was terrifying. And now, exactly the same thing, but it's freeing. So having somebody who can guide that reorientation could be helpful.

F: I called the Zen place that I had been going to and told them what had happened. And I was met with a lot of anger. There was no way it could have happened because I hadn't been sitting long enough. They had a sesshin, but I could only go for two nights of the full week that they had it. For the people that could only go part time, it was just four hours of sitting meditation.

At the time sitting for four hours was absolutely no problem at all for me. They were frustrated because I had to work and because I wasn't ready to give up the world and sit for a week and listen to the Roshi talk about the Buddha. As if my sincerity only showed in certain ways that they deemed appropriate.

So for them, that this had happened to me was insulting. It was almost like they wanted me to come back and get retrained. I was like, "Did I do something wrong here? What happened here?" I didn't go back. I probably should have. But I didn't. I didn't need to go back and be told that I had messed up royally. At the same time I realized this wasn't something they could take away.

J: If there was anybody there who could have provided support and guidance then it seems that they did a disservice by not just letting go of their egos and just recognizing that you really could have used some support.

F: Looking back, some people had been there a long time and it wasn't about seeking any more. It was a social club. And that's fine. But for me it was just that I had no idea what to do. I had no one to talk to about this. All I could do was read the books at the secondhand store.

J: What year was that?

F: 2001.

I contacted someone who had encouraged me to sit at home by myself. I emailed him. He didn't respond. So finally I asked if he'd received my email, and he said, "Yeah. I got it." And I said, "Well, what did you think?" And he said, "What am I supposed to think? It's just an everyday thing, isn't it?" I was insulted by it. I thought he was going to celebrate it. But he didn't.

J: But at the same time, it completely turned your world upside down. It seems to me there's got to be a middle ground. I mean, sure, it's no big deal. But on the other hand, it could have been helpful if someone could have said that this can happen, it's no big deal, but I can offer you a little bit of guidance to help you explore this so that you don't have to drink for the next couple of years.

F: That would have been nice.

It's like listening to some kid who says, "I fell in love. It's the first time I had sex." And you say, "Yeah. That's great." And he says, "No. You don't understand. I just had sex!" "Yeah. I get it. I heard you the first time. I'm old enough to be your father. I know what that's about."

You can understand someone's excitement. But at the same time, it's not a big deal.

J: I can see that. But sometimes I'm talking with someone, and I can see that someone is seeking something - an escape from suffering. I can't offer them support in escaping. So I just keep pointing that there is no possibility of escape. "Give it up. And accept the misery that is your life."

And sometimes when I'm having these conversations, I realize that some of these people are bound to be very disappointed when they finally discover what I'm pointing to. Because it's totally ordinary. It's not a big deal. Not even in the slightest. It's the opposite. Because it's the complete collapse of any big deal.

But at the same time, sometimes people get it and it's a totally easy transition. Whereas for other people it might be a really big deal. Like for you. And I think it's unhelpful not to acknowledge that when that's the case. You know, it would be like if someone's lying on the side of the road with their leg cut off, and people just walk by saying, "Well, it's not that big of a deal because we're all going to die sooner or later."

F: I fell into that for a long time. I felt that nothing mattered. "What's the point? Have another drink."

And for me, stopping drinking was a non-event. It was the culmination of everything that had happened. It was just stopping and I wasn't an alcoholic again. When that fell away, everything else fell away too. The whole nihilistic view fell away. Mountains are mountains again, dammit!

Nihilism

I use the word "nihilism" incorrectly most of the time. Technically, nihilism (or, more precisely, existential nihilism) refers to the philosophy that there is absolutely no meaning inherent in life. Which, as far as philosophy goes, is pretty good. Experientially, I agree.

However, I often use the term nihilism to refer to the phenomenon of the "nothing matters" attitude. Of course, nothing matters. But the question is, are you imagining that nothing matters to or for you? Normally, when we have a "nothing matters" attitude then we are assuming that we are separate selves to whom nothing matters. As though there is some separate you that gets to decide if anything matters. And this sort of nihilism is most definitely not what Fish and I are ultimately pointing to throughout these conversations.

In this conversation we talk about Fish's decade-long drinking strategy and how that may have come about as a failure to see through this sort of "nothing matters" style of nihilism. And then we talk about the ongoing revelation of the truth of nothingness and meaninglessness that manifests as subtle joy.

J: So how long did the drinking go on?

F: About a decade.

J: Really?

F: Well, not hardcore the whole time. But for a while it got really bad. Off and on for a few years, then really bad.

The attitude that I really just didn't give a shit about anything was not conducive to functioning.

J: That only ended a few years ago?

F: About three years ago.

J: That's a long time to be a nihilist.

F: I just didn't give a shit. I really didn't care. It wasn't conducive to working around other people or motivating other people, which is what I was doing just a few years before that. I was used to helping people change their lives. Motivating them to be different and to be better than they were before they came to class. And then I saw the futility of it all. Fuck it. I couldn't wear the facade any longer.

And now, you know what? It's not so bad as I had thought. Now I don't care, but in a different way.

It doesn't sound very romantic when you say, "I really don't care, dude."

J: I have that trouble. I tell people that all the time. And I mean it. And then I hear that as if I was the other person. And I realize that it probably doesn't sound all that good. So then it's like, "It's not the way that you're hearing it. It's just that I honestly don't care."

F: "What if I don't wake up after this talk?"

"Well, I don't care."

Which means that it's not going to affect me one way or the other.

J: Yeah. It's not going to affect anything. The other thing - and this doesn't go over very well - but I realized that compassion, for example - you know that compassion is held out as this really noble thing, especially in Buddhism. And I realized that there's nothing wrong with compassion. I mean, I like compassion, it feels quite nice, but the honest to goodness truth is that it has absolutely no meaning or value whatsoever. Because it's not what you think it is. We're led to think that compassion is this noble, loving energy from one to another. But actually it's just another thing happening. That's it. It doesn't have anything to do with anyone.

F: No. It doesn't. I mean, it might make you feel good. It might make a person feel better that you empathize with them. It doesn't make the situation any different. If something bad happened and you feel bad for them, that doesn't change what happened.

J: The nice thing is that it's much more enjoyable to know that compassion doesn't mean anything. It's interesting to see how something as innocuous and really nice as compassion can turn out to be yet another little trap.

F: Because then if you don't show compassion then you're just a fucking asshole.

J: And people won't like me.

F: "What do you mean you didn't help that person out?"

"Well, I couldn't help that person out because it was out of my skill set."

"Well, you could have at least pretended that you care."

It's like, "I want you to want me," which is a great Cheap Trick song.

J: It's never going to win you a popularity contest. Like you've said before, there's something for everyone out there. So I don't need to be everything for everybody. It's much better, I think, to be completely honest. And then someone who can actually benefit from a relationship with you will be able to find you because you're honest about it. Like saying, "I don't care." And most people will say, "What? He doesn't care? Well, screw him. I'm going to go to this other guy." But then somebody will hear that, and be like, "Wow! I've been looking for somebody who doesn't care, forever."

F: No matter how shitty the song is on the radio, for somebody that's his or her life theme. There's somebody out there who's marching to that song. And you're like, "Dude! That's the worst song ever." And they say, "Yeah, but it's everything in my life!" And you're like, "Are you serious?"

And if you told a musician, "I hate you. I hate your music. I hate the way you play guitar," then the musician would say, "Well, go listen to somebody else. I'm not going to change my music." Unless he's a sell out. "I'm not going to change my music just so you'll buy my CD or my DVD. Go listen to some other guy. Don't come and shit on my parade."

J: Metallica's already got plenty of fans.

F: Exactly. This is how I get my point across. And if you don't like it, then go listen to somebody else. Don't tell me how it should be.

The Final Word

From Fish:

Dear seeker/loser,

    I hope that you both enjoyed the dialogue between Joey and me and that it angered you as well. I know some folks will get butt-hurt over the language I use sometimes, but that's just too fucking bad. I'm no savior or saint and I'm not here to make you feel good about yourself. I prefer a direct, in your face and sometimes angry approach to things and sometimes that's painful.
    There are too many "spiritual" books out there that confuse us and make this something mystical and almost impossible to attain. Those teachings are filled with flowery language that only frustrates us because we start to believe that we are somehow impure and must be better people to become enlightened.
    Our dialogue smashes the notion that you have to be a new age vegetarian filled with sappy love, hugs and the notion that violence never solves anything. You don't need to wear hippy vests, beads or smell like patchouli (unless you want blind people to hate you too) for enlightenment to happen.

Enlightenment doesn't happen because you are already this and always have been.

If you do happen to become angry while reading this, ask yourself why. Are you ready to pull out your internet bookmarks (which are right there next to your porn and online gaming strategies) and send them to me to point out my errors? Did I make fun of the stupid things you believe you'll get when you're enlightened? Did you recognize some of my stupid fantasies as your own and now you feel like an exposed asshole? Good.

Maybe you'll direct your energy into looking into this, just as it is, without your unnecessary commentary, beliefs, permissions or selfish desires. Stop running away from this into an imaginary that. It never works.

Strip everything away until there is nothing left.

Feel free to contact me at scrapperzen101@gmail.com.

From Joey:

I always have to have the last word. And as the editor I get to do whatever I want. So here I get to have the final say.

My sincere hope is that this book has taken something from you. I hope that it has made it impossible for you to believe in some of the painful assumptions that had, up to now, made life seem unbearable and lonely.

We live in a culture that likes to leave us feeling good. Which isn't hard to do. It's a cheap trick. Have a cookie; you'll probably feel better. Or we could end the book with some nice words that suggest that you're about to get it and be done with the things you don't like forever.

And maybe you'd feel better for a few minutes. Or an hour. Maybe until tomorrow. And then the state would pass. Because states always pass.

So I prefer to leave you with nothing. At least as best as possible, I prefer to take everything from you. And that may feel lousy. Maybe even depressing, which is good. Because if temporary "feel good" fixes haven't worked, then at least you have to admit that this is something different.

In conclusion, let me remind you that you'll never get it. You'll never escape what you want to escape from. You'll never get rid of problems. You'll never get rid of the messiness of life. Pain will still happen. Some people will continue to dislike you. It's unlikely that Jesus, Krishna or Buddha will start speaking to you. And even if they do, it's meaningless. Just like everything else.

Give it all up. Stop trying. Stop entirely. Let go. Drop everything. Don't touch a thing. And discover yourself as you are, in all your horror and wonder and everything else.

I invite you to email me at joeylott@gmail.com if you have any questions, doubts, comments or anything else.

Happiness Made Simple E-Course

I hope that you have enjoyed this book. If so, then I'd like to invite you to read my Happiness Made Simple E-Course. In this completely free e-course you will discover just how easy true happiness is. Instead of arduous affirmations, techniques, and visualizations, in this E-Course you'll learn how to tune in to the effortless happiness that is already here when only you know how to look.

Sign up for free at my website, www.joeylott.com. When you do, you'll begin receiving Happiness Made Simple in a series of emails delivered directly to your inbox. This E-Course comes with no strings attached. I promise you there are no sleazy internet marketing hooks involved. You have my word.

Connect With Me

I welcome your questions, comments, and feedback of any kind. Please feel free to email me at joeylott@gmail.com. I am now receiving so many emails that I cannot always reply to every email. I do read them all, and I do my best to reply to as many as possible. For the benefit of others, I may choose to publish my response to your email on my blog or in book format. I will maintain your privacy and anonymity if I choose to publish my response.

One Small Favor

My sincere goal in writing is to share something that may be of value to you. And I endeavor to do so while keeping the costs low for readers. The success of my books and my ability to reach other readers who may benefit from my books depends in large part on having lots of thoughtful, honest reviews written about my work. You would do me a great favor if you would please take a moment to generously write a review of this book at Amazon.com. This will only take a few minutes of your time, and you will be helping me a great deal. I sure would appreciate it.

About the Author

"The secret to happiness is to let go of everything - see through every assumption."

Beginning at a young age Joey Lott experienced intensifying anxiety. For several decades he lived with restrictive eating disorders, obsessions, compulsions, and an inescapable fear. By the time he was 30 years old he was physically sick, emotionally volatile, and mentally obsessed with keeping any and all unwanted thoughts and experiences at bay.

At this time Lott was living on a futon mattress in a tiny cabin in the woods. He was so sick that he could barely move. He was deeply depressed and hopeless. All this despite doing all the "right" things such as years of meditation, yoga, various "perfect" diets, clean air, and pure water.

Just when things were at their most dire, a crack appeared in the conceptual world that had formerly been mistaken for reality. By peering into this crack and underneath all the assumptions that had been unquestioned up to that moment, Lott began a great undoing. The revelation of this undoing is that reality is utterly simple, ever-present, seamless, and indivisible.

Lott's books provide a glimpse into the seamless, simple, and joyous nature of reality, offering a glimpse through the crack in conceptual worlds. Whether writing about the ultimate non-dual nature of reality, eating disorders, stress, disease, or any other subject, he offers the invitation to look at things differently, leaving behind the old, out-grown, painful limitations we have used to bind ourselves in suffering. And then, he welcomes you home to the effortless simplicity of yourself as you are.

Not sure where to begin? Pick up a copy of Lott's most popular book, *You're Trying Too Hard*, which strips away all the concepts that keep us searching for a greater, more spiritual, more peaceful life or self.

Made in the USA
Middletown, DE
28 July 2018